1
2

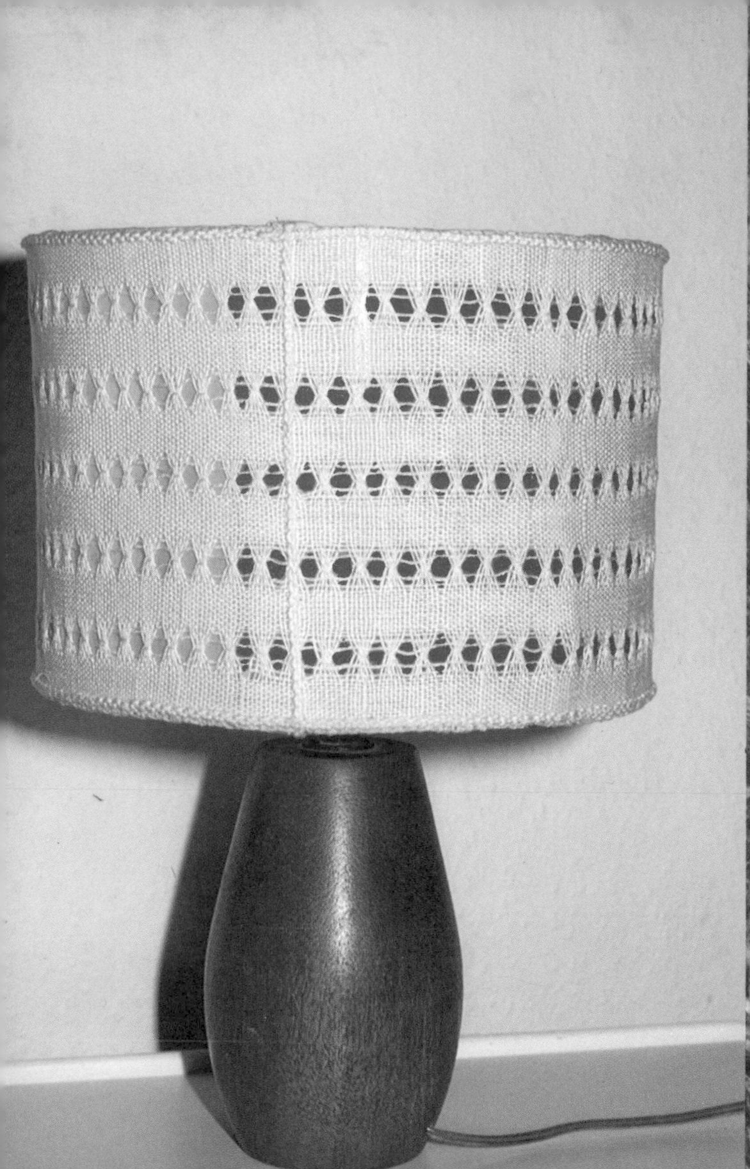
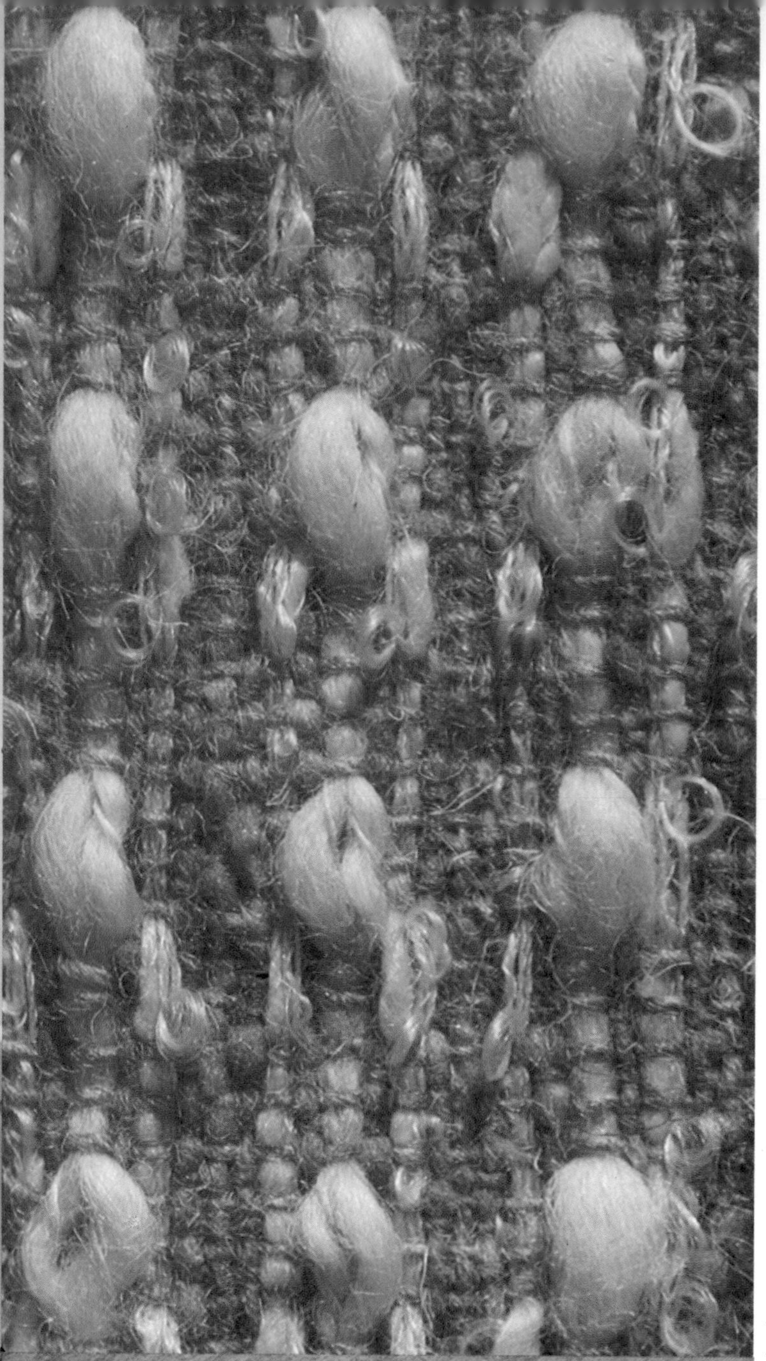

35
46

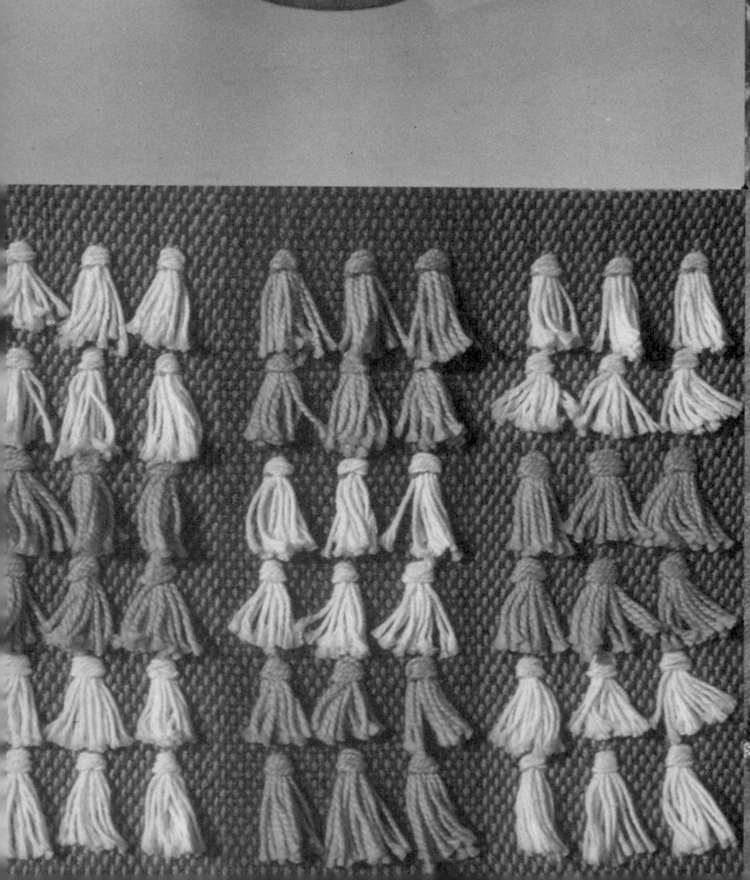
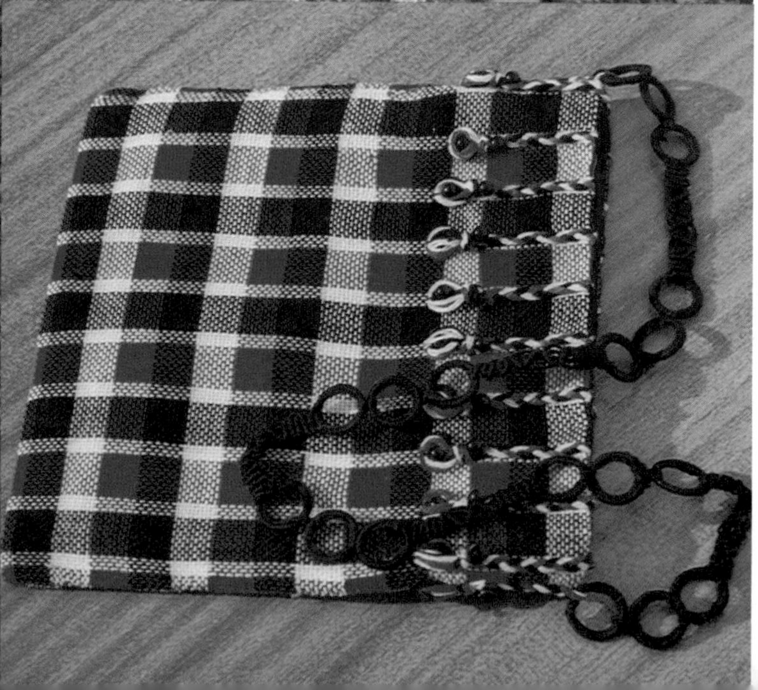

7

8
11
9
12
10

Practical
Modern Weaving

ROSEMARY MURRAY

 VAN NOSTRAND REINHOLD COMPANY
New York   Cincinnati   Toronto   London   Melbourne

Van Nostrand Reinhold Company Regional Offices:
New York Cincinnati Chicago Millbrae Dallas

Van Nostrand Reinhold Company International offices:
London Toronto Melbourne

Library of Congress Catalog Card Number 74–9189
ISBN 0–442–30077–8 (cl.)
ISBN 0–442–30078–6 (pb.)

This book is filmset in Century Schoolbook and
printed in Great Britain by Jolly & Barber Ltd., Rugby.

Designed by Rod Josey Associates

Published by Van Nostrand Reinhold Company Inc.,
450 West 33rd Street, New York, N.Y. 10001 and
Van Nostrand Reinhold Company Ltd.,
Molly Millars Lane, Wokingham, Berkshire, England.

16 15 14 13 12 11 10 9 8 7 6 5 4 3 2 1

Library of Congress Cataloging in Publication Data
Murray, Rosemary.
Practical modern weaving.
Bibliography: p.
Includes index.
1. Hand weaving. I. Title.
TT848.M87   746.1'4   74–9189
ISBN 0–442–30077–8
ISBN 0–442–30078–6 pbk.

Acknowledgements

Captions to Colour Plates

Colour plate 1. This group includes a cushion cover, smock yoke and waste paper basket in monksbelt, a traycloth in goose eye, two lengths of furnishing fabric, a small tapestry and a sunflower pin cushion woven on a card loom.

Colour plate 2. A printed warp.

Colour plate 3. Lampshade with lace ovals on a spaced warp, mounted on coloured acetate.

Colour plate 4. An example of decorative knotting.

Colour plate 5. Deep-textured woollen fabric.

Colour plate 6. The cross check fabric for this bag was done in plain weave on a 2-way loom.

Colour plate 7. Detail of a fringe: knotted pile on a plain weave.

Colour plate 8. Tapestry hanging woven on a 4-shaft loom.

Colour plate 9. Tapestry striped bag with tassels, worked on a 2-way loom in cotton, double knit woollens, Aran yarn and carpet thrums.

Colour plate 10. Bag in vertical slit tapestry.

Colour plate 11. Detail of a red lectern cloth. The warp of 12/2 cotton (28 dent) is in various shades of red, brown and purple. The weft is thick wool and fancy yarn. The rectangles of copper and gold lurex were worked with interlocked wefts. This is really a tapestry technique, but was used on this cloth with normal beating.

Colour plate 12. Wall hanging using skip plain weave. This is another tapestry technique, normally used with close beating.

Colour plate 13. Hanging in Spanish lace and knotting.

Colour plate 14. Batik printed strip weave on a spaced warp.

Colour plate 15. Hanging woven with slits; macramé has been worked over the warp strands. Made on a 2-way loom.

Colour plate 16. Hanging woven with a spaced warp and employing macramé and beads.

Colour plate 17. 'The Red Queen'. This uses most of the techniques described in the tapestry section.

I would like to thank the Chief Education Officer of the County Borough of Southend-on-Sea and the Headmistress of Belfairs High School for Girls, Leigh-on-Sea, for permission to use photographs of students' work. Thanks are also due to Brian Murray for his photographic work, and to my students, past and present, whose work I am proud to include in this book.

Contents

Introduction

THE MORE PLASTIC and pre-wrapped our society becomes, the more people turn to handicrafts as a means of aesthetic realization. Today there is a growing interest in handweaving, but it is not always possible for the would-be weaver to find personal instruction. This book, therefore, is written for the amateur with no previous experience of weaving. It is also intended as an introductory work for teachers. The technical instructions are easily understandable, based on experience of teaching weaving to others. *Practical Modern Weaving* is also an ideas book and the suggestions outlined in it use only the simplest equipment and methods. Many of the illustrations are the work of girls in school.

The handicraftsman can never compete with the power loom in terms of speed, cheapness and technical perfection. His aim should be to experiment, to try varied techniques using the traditions of the past in a different way. The practical weaver will find ideas in the book for simple and useful articles, while others may use the loom as a means of self expression, executing small tapestries, wall hangings and three dimensional forms valued for their decorative qualities alone. Some suggestions employ other skills such as embroidery, macramé, printing and tie-dyeing combined with weaving.

The aim of the book is principally to instruct, and at the same time to provide starting points for personal exploration, leaving the individual free to develop original ideas of colour, texture, pattern and shape.

1. What is Weaving?

IN CROCHET AND KNITTING cloth is formed by looping one thread around itself. In weaving, on the other hand, the fabric is made by interlacing two sets of threads, known as the *warp* and the *weft*. The warp is the foundation on which the cloth is made and consists of threads stretched lengthwise on a frame, which is called the *loom*. The threads which interlace across the *warp*, from side to side, form the *weft*. The *weave* is the way in which these two sets of threads interlace.

Fig. 1–1. *Weaving on a lampshade ring* (opposite).

Fig. 1–2. *Another example of weaving on a lampshade ring.*

Fig. 1–3. Wind chimes made by weaving on a lampshade ring in gimp and plastic raffia.

The simplest form of weaving is *darning,* the hole in the cloth forming the *loom* and the initial stitches, taken across the hole, the *warp.* The *weft* is woven by another thread passing at right angles under and over the warp threads on a needle. This darning technique forms the basis of all primitive weaving techniques.

There are many ways of weaving without using a conventional loom. Preliminary experiments can be carried out by devising looms from picture frames, nails driven into a board, cardboard shapes with teeth cut into the edges holding the warp, and firm wire rings or wheels (Figs. 1–1, 1–2 and 1–3). Small branches of trees, rods arranged to form a frame, and twisted wire armatures can also be used to support threads. Appendix B tells you how to weave on rings.

Before starting to weave it is helpful to examine different kinds of weave intersection. One simple way to do this is to take a sheet of card or cardboard, cut it into strips and pin the strips on to a drawing board; another set of strips is then woven across the first set. By using strongly contrasting colours, emphasis will focus on the interaction of warp and weft and the possibilities open to

you will become apparent. Explore as many different types of intersections as possible, using this method.

The Language of Weaving

You will already have noticed that weaving has a language of its own, and in order to follow the instructions in this book you will need to become familiar with the meaning of weaving terms. The two key words *warp* and *weft* have been explained, and other unfamiliar words and expressions will be defined and explained as they occur in the text, and also in the *Glossary* on page 108. Whenever you are doubtful about the meaning of a weaving term, refer to this *Glossary.*

Definition of a Loom

After experimenting with your makeshift 'looms' you will wish to consider using a conventional loom; in other words, a frame specifically designed to make weaving quick and easy.

All looms have basic principles in common, with adjustable rollers front and back to enable cloth to be made that

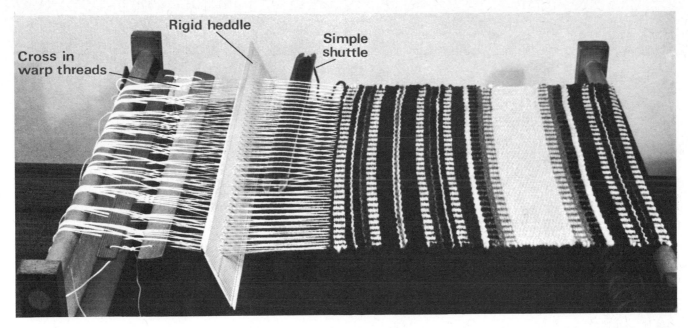

Fig. 1–4. Two-way loom with rigid heddle. On the loom is the tapestry weave for the bag in Colour plate 9.

is longer than the length of the loom. The darning process, going under and over the warp threads with the weft thread on a needle, is replaced by a device which, in one movement, separates the warp threads into two layers. The triangular space created between the two layers of thread is called the *shed*, and the weft thread is then passed between these two layers.

Choosing a Loom

There are many different types of loom on the market, but this book concentrates only on the two looms most suitable for the novice: the 2-way loom with a rigid heddle, and the 4-shaft table loom. *(The 2-shaft table loom is dealt with briefly in Appendix E.)*

2-Way Loom with Rigid Heddle. This inexpensive loom is strong, easy to use, light to handle and convenient to

store (Fig. 1–4). It has rollers back and front which enable a long warp to be set up. The main limitations of this loom are that only plain weave can be woven on it and fine cloth cannot be woven at all. However, remember that work in simple weaves need never be dull and that many of the techniques and patterns described further on in the book can be worked on a 2-way loom.

4-Shaft Table Loom. With the 4-shaft table loom there is a much greater degree of flexibility, the *shafts* making possible a wide variety of patterns and the separate *reed* (Fig. 1–5) permitting a wide range of *setts (number of warp threads per inch)*.

This type of loom is more expensive and less mobile than the 2-way loom; it also requires more storage space. Nevertheless, this is my first choice for the beginner as a wide range of patterns can be executed on it, and exciting experiments can be carried out on it, allowing for expansion of knowledge and growth of experience. The 4-shaft loom might appear to be more complicated to use than the 2-way loom, but in practice this is not the case. Followed step-by-step, the procedure for mounting a warp on to the loom is simple, the movement of front and back rollers is easy to adjust, and correct *beating* (firming of the weft) easy to achieve.

Fig. 1–5. Four-shaft table loom.
A. The front roller or cloth beam. The cloth is rolled on this when it is woven.
B. The back roller or warp beam on which the warp is wound. Both rollers are controlled by a ratchet and pawl.
C. These are made of wire or string with a hole or loop in the middle of each, through which the warp threads are passed. This loop is called an eye.
D. This is the reed, a metal comb with vertical grooves called dents in it. The reed is used for spacing the warp and beating up the rows of weaving.
E. The swinging wooden frame holding the reed.
F. A shuttle.
G. The harness, shaft or frame. Wooden or metal frames hold the heddles. There are four on this Harris table loom. When the levers are used, the shafts rise to form a shed. This is the triangular space made when a warp is divided into two layers. The shuttle, carrying the weft thread, passes through the shed.

15

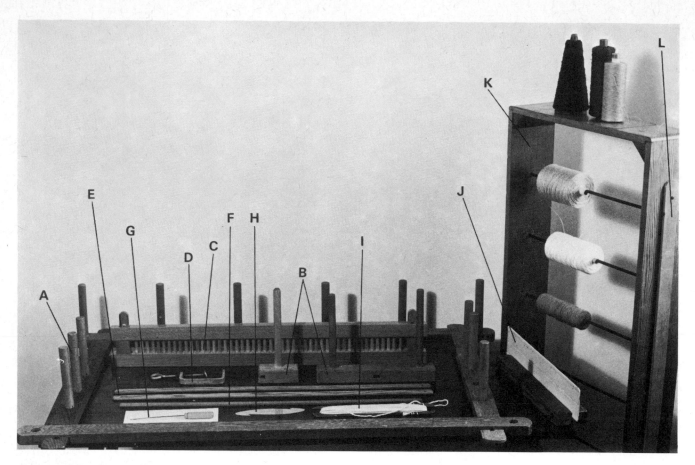

Other Equipment

As well as your loom you will need to acquire some other small items of equipment.

Warping frame (Figs. 1–6A and 3–4) with movable pegs.

Warping posts (Fig. 1–6B), clamped with *G-clamps* (Fig. 1–6D) to a table.

Raddle (Fig. 1–6C) for spreading the warp before threading the loom.

Cross sticks (Fig. 1–6E) for placing through crossed warp threads, to keep them in order.

Warp sticks (Fig. 1–6F) for placing between rows of warp threads as the warp is being wound on to the back beam.

Threading hook (Fig. 1–6G): small hook, used for threading the warp.

Reed hook (Fig. 1–6H): hook used for threading the warp through the spaces in the reed.

Shuttles (Fig. 1–6I) used for carrying the weft thread.

Bobbin winder and bobbins (Fig. 6–2): necessary only if a roller or boat shuttle is used (see page 33).

Spool racks (Fig. 1–6K): useful refinements for holding the yarn while warping; however they are not essential.

Clamp for holding the heddle on a 2-way loom.

Fig. 1–6. Other small items of equipment.
A. Warping frame or warping board.
B. Single and double warping posts.
C. Raddle.
D. G-clamp.
E. Cross sticks.
F. Warp stick or rolling on stick.
G. Threading hook.
H. Reed hook.
I. Simple shuttle.
J. Rigid heddle (heddle reed) held in heddle holder or clamp.
K. Spool rack. To place spools on the rack raise the side bar (L) and slip the steel rod through the centre of the spool.

2. Learning about Yarns

YARNS COME FROM BOTH NATURAL and synthetic fibres. The natural fibres may be divided into two groups: vegetable and animal. The four main natural fibres are wool, cotton, linen and silk.

Natural Fibres

Cotton. This is the ideal yarn for the beginner as it is strong, elastic and easy to handle. Mistakes in the weave are easy to spot because the interlacement of threads shows clearly. Cotton comes in a great variety of colours and can be purchased in small quantities (in 8 oz. *cheeses*: Fig. 2–1). It is also available in many different thicknesses. *Mercerization (treatment with caustic soda)* adds to its strength, makes it glossy, and increases its dye absorption.

Fig. 2–1. Packages of yarn, showing wool and linen cheeses, cotton cones, skeins of plastic raffia and a ball of sisal.

Wool. Wool comes from the fleece of the sheep and other wool-bearing animals and is, without doubt, the handweaver's favourite yarn. Like cotton, it is strong and elastic and comes in a wide range of colours. It is advisable to use wool which has been specially made for handweaving, but knitting wools can be used instead.

Linen. Linen is a more difficult yarn to use than cotton or wool. It is a strong yarn but lacks elasticity and is, therefore, brittle to use. At the warping and threading stage it is springy and slippery and on the loom tensioning presents problems (damping the warp ends before tying helps).

Silk. Silk is a most difficult material for handweavers to handle, and only experienced handweavers should contemplate using this yarn.

Synthetics

Synthetic fibres are made from many different substances: wood, petroleum, cellulose, coal and so on. Although they are not so pleasant to handle as natural yarns, their strength, brilliance of colour and relatively low cost make them an attractive proposition to the weaver.

Fancy Yarns

(Fig. 2–2. Colour plate 5.)

A large variety of fancy yarns, both natural and synthetic, can be used for decoration in the weft. Some of these yarns are not strong, and it is not therefore advisable to use them for the warp, which is constantly under tension. Test the strength of these yarns, if you want to use them in a *warp*, by pulling them between your hands. To make a firm cloth with thin fancy yarns throughout the *weft*, use a stronger yarn in each pick, together with your fancy yarn.

Fig. 2–2. A selection of fancy yarns. From left to right: worsted slub, wool loop, worsted monstryl slub bouclé, three chenilles, four gimps, slub and mohair.

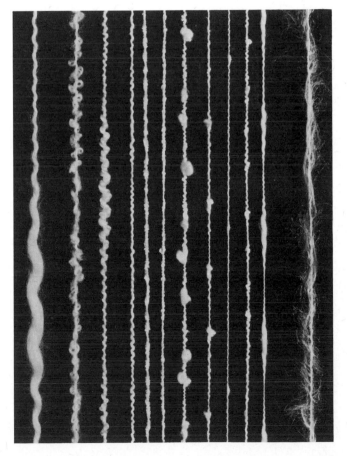

C

The Count of Yarn

In the *fixed weight system*, yarn is classified according to its yardage per pound. (See Appendix G for the system known as *Tex,* which will eventually replace the fixed weight system.) The number designated to the yarn is called the *count*. A thick yarn obviously has less length per pound and carries a low count number; conversely, a fine yarn contains more yardage per pound and carries a higher number. This system operates for all the natural yarns used in this book.

low count number = thick yarn
high count number = thinner yarn.

Cotton. The standard measurement for cotton is 840 yards, i.e. a cotton classified as 1 contains 1 hank of 840 yards per pound. A cotton classified as 6 contains 840 × 6 yards per pound (5,040 yards per pound), i.e. 6 hanks.

A strand of yarn used alone is termed a *singles*; two or more single threads twisted together form a *ply*. If the yarn is plied, the number of strands twisted together is shown alongside the original count (as a rule it is the smaller number), and the two figures are separated by an oblique stroke. Generally the yarn comes first, but occasionally the ply number is placed first: 2/6 (or 2/6s or 6/2 or 6/2s) means that a yarn of 6 count (840 yards × 6) has been plied double, making the final count 3 (840 yards × 3 per pound), i.e. 2,520 yards in a pound.

Wool. In Great Britain the system varies between the different wool areas. The *skein* system in Yorkshire uses a base of 256 yards per pound to the skein, making 256 yards per pound of raw wool the standard for a number 1 singles yarn. The *cut* system in Scottish yarn (Galashiels) uses a base of 200 yards to the cut, making 200 yards per pound of raw wool the standard for a number 1 singles yarn. These singles tweed yarns are oily, which makes them strong enough for weaving; the oil disappears when the cloth is washed (see Appendix A). The system for knitting wools is based on the *ply*. Using the same singles yarn, twisting together 2 strands (2 ply) will make a finer wool than 3 or 4 ply.

In the United States the *cut* system uses a base of 300 yards to the cut, making 300 yards per pound of raw wool the standard for a number 1 singles yarn. In the *American run* system, 1,600 yards per pound of raw wool is the standard count for a number 1 yarn.

Linen. The yardage count of linen is based on a unit called a *lea,* which is 300 yards long. The count depends on the number of 300 yard hanks in a pound of yarn. If the yarn is plied it is shown as in cotton, e.g. 8/2 is an 8 yarn with 2 strands plied; 4 × 300 = 1,200 yards per pound.

Collecting Yarn

All weaving begins with yarn, so collect as wide a range as possible. Most households have odd balls of wool and string, as well as old sweaters which can be unpicked in order to use the wool. Experiment with all your odd pieces of yarn, arranging it in harmonizing and contrasting groups. Observe what happens when one yarn is twisted round another. Wind wool on strips of card and consider the proportion of the stripes; then darn colours across the bound sections and study the colour combinations you have used and the effect of one colour upon another.

Stockists will supply yarn in small quantities (see *Suppliers*). Fancy yarn varies in quantities according to its bulk: some are sold in 1 oz. skeins, others in 8 oz. skeins. The range of colours offered is very wide but it is more economical to buy undyed yarn and dye it at home. Singles tweed yarn generally comes in larger quantities than cotton: 1–1½ lb. is the average weight offered. Some stockists, however, supply skeins of wool suitable for weaving. For tapestry, thicker wool in broken ranges of colour can be bought cheaply from carpet firms. When ordering broken hanks it is advisable to say that the yarn is for weaving, to avoid cut hanks being put in the order to make up the exact weight.

When making your initial order ask for a small number of yarns of various thicknesses and colours. Mercerized cotton in 4/2 or 6/2 (similar to 3 ply wool in thickness) is a useful weight to start with; so is 11 cut in tweed singles, which is an oily wool, strong enough for warps as well as weft. Thin and heavier fancy yarns, for surface texture, can be ordered in natural colour and dyed to blend or contrast as you wish.

When you have a reasonable collection of yarns, make a selection, ranging from fine cotton to strips cut from old woollens and stockings or tights, and dye them all in the same dye bath. Some of the results will surprise you, as dyes react quite differently on different materials.

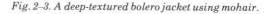

Fig. 2–3. A deep-textured bolero jacket using mohair.

3. Starting Off – Warping

WHEN PREPARING A LOOM for weaving, a logical sequence must be followed. At first glance, the processes may seem complicated and long-winded, but they are really very simple. Remember to take each set of instructions slowly, and study the illustrations which accompany the text very carefully. Persevere, and the instructions will soon become clear to you. By the time you have completed two pieces of cloth, the routine of setting up a loom and weaving will no longer appear difficult. Remember that all crafts, if they are to be properly mastered, present a series of techniques to be studied and assimilated. If you need encouragement, look at the illustrations of work carried out by my young school students. They mastered the techniques described in this book without difficulty, and so will you if you allow a little time to study the instructions.

Making a Warp

First Calculations. Your initial decision will concern the length and width of your first piece of cloth. I recommend that your first piece should be 20 in. long and 9 in. wide, and the calculations explained in this section are based on these figures. Measurements and calculations have all been worked out in inches. (See Appendix H for metric conversion.)

How to Calculate the Length of a Warp. If your first piece of weaving, therefore, is planned as 20 in. long, your next step will be to calculate the extra yarn required for *warping*. Extra thread is required for:
(1) Tie-ups at the front and back of the loom.
(2) Take-up of yarn caused by the warp and weft threads bending over each other as the cloth is made.

As a beginner you should allow a generous amount of yarn for wastage due to the tie-ups (about 15 in.). You should also make an additional allowance of 6 in. for a *sampler* (the part of the warp used to try out ideas before taking final decisions). Finally, you must make an additional allowance of 4 in. in every 36 in. for take-up.

Example

Length of finished article	20 in.
Wastage (due to tie-ups)	15 in.
Sampler	6 in.
Take-up (of warp)	8 in.
Length of warp	49 in.

How to Calculate the Width of a Warp. When calculating how much yarn will be required for the width of the warp, you must also make an allowance for contraction of the warp, due to take-up of the threads during weaving. The pulling in of the warp depends on three factors: the type of yarn used, the type of pattern used, and the weaver. As a guide, allow a minimum of 1 in. on your first piece of weaving, for cotton. After you have finished weaving check whether the allowance was sufficient.

Example

Finished width required	9 in.
Take-up	1 in.
	10 in.

How to Calculate the Number of Ends in a Warp. The length and width of your warp have now been calculated and your next task will be to calculate how many threads your warp will contain (the individual warp threads are referred to as *ends*). As we have established, your first piece of weaving will have a warp width of 10 in. (9 in. + 1 in. take-up) and you should calculate the ends required as follows:

2-way loom: the rigid heddle (Fig. 1–4) carries 13 ends to the inch. Simply multiply the proposed width (9 in.) + take-up (1 in.) by the number of ends per inch (13) to arrive at the number of ends needed for the warp, i.e. $10 \times 13 = 130$. Two threads are doubled at each side for the selvedge, making a final total of 130 + 4 ends.

4-shaft loom: the number of ends will depend on the proposed width of cloth + density of cloth. For the first piece choose a 14 *dent reed* (see page 71 and the *Glossary*) which will give 14 ends to the inch. Therefore multiply the proposed width (9 in.) + take-up (1 in.) by 14 and add 8 threads for selvedge (4 at each side), which brings the total to 148.

Preparing the Yarn for Warping. You are now in a position to make the warp. This could be done by cutting lengths of yarn and tying each one on to the loom, but this would be a slow and tedious task. Instead, the warp is made in one long loop of yarn, and the threads are held in their correct order by twisting them round posts in the shape of a figure eight.

There are many different methods of *warping (preparing the warp threads for weaving)*; to make this process easy, it is best to use a special piece of equipment. On the following pages instructions are given for warping on *warping posts,* and for warping on a *frame or board* (when a longer piece of weaving is planned).

For this first piece of weaving I suggest that you use *warping posts* (Fig. 1–6B), as you will find these simpler to start with.

Choice of Yarn. As already stated, it is advisable to choose cotton for your warp, until you have gained some experience. For this first piece, order a strong mercerized cotton, either 4/2 or 6/2, and choose a medium shade. You should allow 2 oz. for a warp of this length (see Appendix C *Estimating Weight of Yarn for Warp and Weft*).

If you are winding the warp from spools these should be placed on spool racks; skeins should be wound into balls, and each ball put into a large jar to prevent it rolling on the floor. Cones can be used on the floor. The yarn will then reel smoothly off the top and there will be no danger of it becoming tangled.

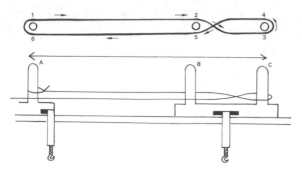

Fig. 3–1. Making the warp.

Single Warping on Posts. Look carefully at Fig. 3–1 and then set up the warping posts 49 in. apart to accommodate your warp length of 49 in. (from A to C). Tie the end of the yarn to the single post A with a double knot. Reel the yarn smoothly and twist it round the warping posts, following the diagram. Take it behind peg B (2), round C (3 and 4), across to the front of B (5), and back to A (6). From peg A to peg C is one warp end; when you have returned to A, therefore, you will have made 2 warp ends. Continue like this until the correct number of ends have been warped.

Try not to put threads on top of one another but give them some space on the pegs, and push them down when the pegs are full.

Counting the Warp. To avoid losing count, loop a different coloured yarn around groups of threads as you wind. This marking can be done at the cross round the number of threads to an inch (i.e. 14 per inch for a 4-way loom). If you do need to check, twist the end of the warp yarn round the single post twice, to keep it taut, then count the threads at one side of the long loop, and double the number. (Remember to make a note of the number you have warped if you have to leave it unfinished.)

Importance of the Cross. The crossing of the threads between the double posts (Fig. 3–2) is important because it places the ends in the correct sequence for threading. Great care is needed in securing this order before the warp is taken from the posts. Either take a thin string through both loops of the cross, right round the cross, or put the cross sticks in position while the warp is still on the table; the second method is advisable for beginners. To make the tie joining the cross sticks follow Figs. 3–3a and b. Push

Fig. 3–2. The cross in the warp, on the warping posts.

the sticks fairly close together so that the holes in the ends come opposite one another. Pass each end of a piece of thin string downwards through these two holes. Bring one end of the string to the inside, and the other to the outside of the length of string joining the sticks between the holes. Make a firm double knot over the loop, leaving the sticks parallel to each other and a finger's width apart.

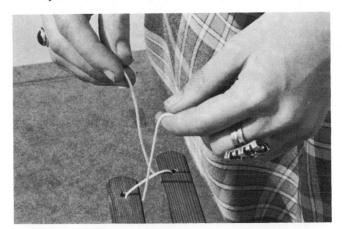

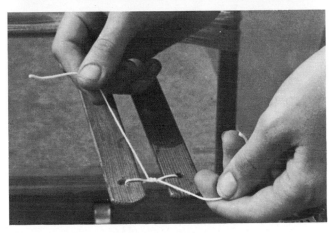

Figs. 3–3a and b. How to tie the cross sticks together (above).

Warping on a Frame or Board. A warping board is more convenient for making longer warps, and it can either be placed on a table or hung from a wall. The warp is taken backwards and forwards across the board instead of along the length of a table (Fig. 3–4).

Fig. 3–4. Warping frame or board. A wooden frame set with movable pegs for warping.

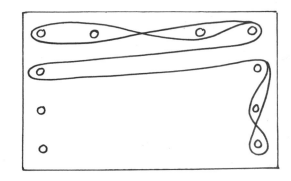

Use of Two Crosses in a Warp. Provided adequate care is taken in making and handling the warp, short lengths can be made with a single cross. But if the warp is long, and particularly if wool is used, a second cross is a wise safeguard. To make a 2-cross warp, arrange a double set of posts or pegs on a frame at the beginning and end of the warp. Cross the threads twice and secure both crosses before chaining. (This process is described in detail in Appendix A.)

Chaining the Warp

When the warping is complete, pull the loop off post A and hold it taut with your left hand. Put your right hand through the loop, and rest the loop on your right wrist; then grasp both sides of the warp and draw the warp through the loop like a crochet chain (Fig. 3–5). This will prevent any tangling of the warp.

Fig. 3–5. Chaining from a warping board.

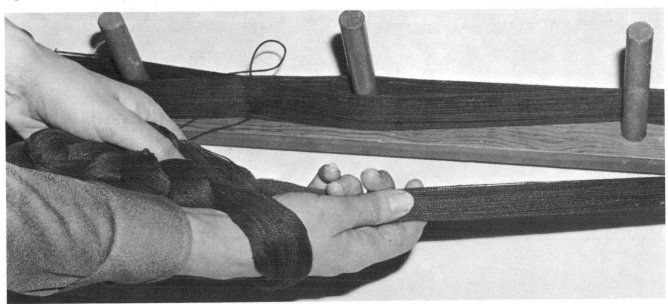

Fig. 3–6. Raddling. Finding the middle of the warp.

Raddling

Dividing the Warp into Two Equal Parts. When you have finished chaining, lay the chained warp flat on a table, with the short loops towards you. To find the middle of the chain, pull the ends, in loops, to each side (Fig. 3–6). Start at the right, and, picking up the part of the loop which is over the cross stick nearest to you, pull it gently outwards to the right. This loop is two ends of the warp (where you tied on and tied off on the warping posts you will have a small loop on a single end: treat this single end in the same way as the doubles). Separate about 10 loops before working in the same way from the left. Nearing the centre, take ends in pairs until you actually reach the centre.

Spreading the Warp on the Raddle. The raddle is a spacer used to spread out the warp to a planned width (Figs. 3–7—3–10). Put the raddle, with its top removed, on the table between you and the warp, with the short loops of the warp facing you. Untie the *warp stick (rolling on stick)* from the back of the loom and place it on the table in front of the raddle. Most raddles have 2 spaces for

every inch, and the warp ends must be placed in those spaces according to the *dent* (threads per inch).

2-way loom: your warp is designed to carry 13 ends per inch and these 13 ends must occupy 2 spaces in some way. To avoid cutting a loop and shortening 2 ends of your warp, let the raddle hold 26 ends over 2 in. (4 spaces). Place 12 ends (6 loops) in the first space, working from the centre. Then miss a space, place 14 ends in the third space and miss out the fourth space. Remember to include the extra selvedge threads in the end spacing.

4-shaft loom: for your first piece of work on a 4-shaft loom you will be raddling for 14 dent. Place the ends in groups of 14 to the inch (6 in the first space, 8 in the next), or in groups of 14 in alternate spaces (Fig. 3–7). As you bring the loop through the space in the raddle, slip it on to the warp stick, taking care not to twist the loop (Fig. 3–8). Continue to the end, and remember to include the extra selvedge ends in the end spacing: return to the centre, and raddle the other side.

It is essential that raddling be carried out with great care and precision. When finding the sequence of ends always look at the threads as they lie between the cross sticks and take the order of threading from that sequence (Fig. 3–9). Ignore any apparent tangles further away from the cross. If the cross itself appears to be in confusion the

Fig. 3–7. The warp is being placed in every other space in the raddle. Seven loops or 14 threads in every other space, or 3 loops, 6 threads and 4 loops, 8 threads using each space, will raddle 14 dent.

Fig. 3–8. Raddling. Slipping the warp loops on to a warp stick.

Fig. 3–9. Raddling. Finding the correct warp thread (below).

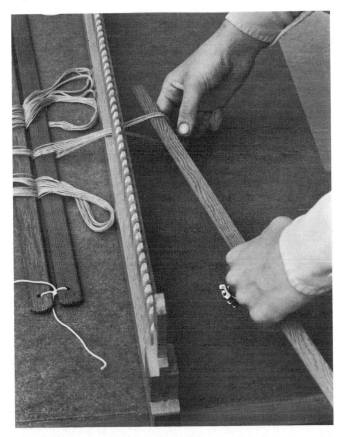

23

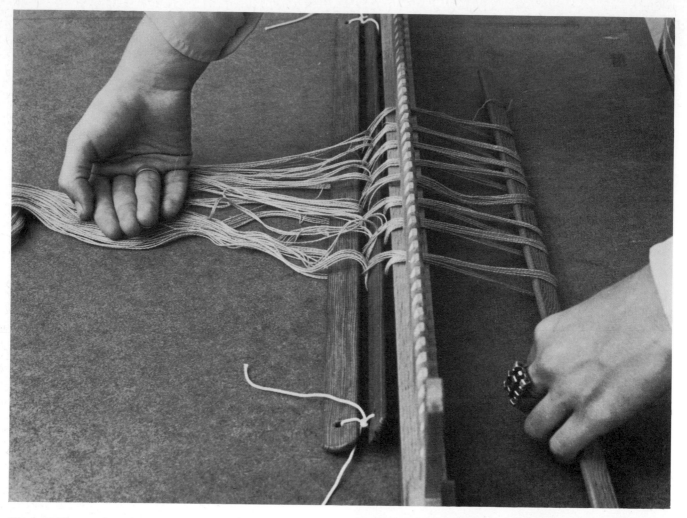

Fig. 3–10. The warp is on the raddle. The hand holding the stick is pulled away from the hand holding the rest of the warp flat on the table. This will smooth out any tangled threads in the cross.

probable explanation is that some threads have worked loose. If this is the case, put your left hand down flat on top of the part of the warp at the far side of the cross; then, holding the loop ends of the warp in your right hand, pull gently while keeping the pressure on the warp with your left hand (Fig. 3–10). This will help the threads to go back to their correct positions.

When all the warp is through the raddle and on the warp stick, put the top on the raddle and secure it with a small peg through the hole at each side (Fig. 3–11).

Tying the Warp on to the Back Beam. Now you are ready to tie the warp on to the *back beam*. (The back of the loom is at the opposite end to where the reed is.) Lift the raddle, together with the warp, to the back of the loom and tie it on to the back beam (Fig. 3–12). Leave a finger's width between the stick in the *apron (the cloth at the front and back of the loom)* and the stick holding the warp. Tie up with knots (Figs. 3–13a, b and c), side knots first, and then place the other knots evenly, taking care not to disturb the straight line of the yarn from the back beam to the raddle.

Fig. 3–11. Pegging the raddle top (right).

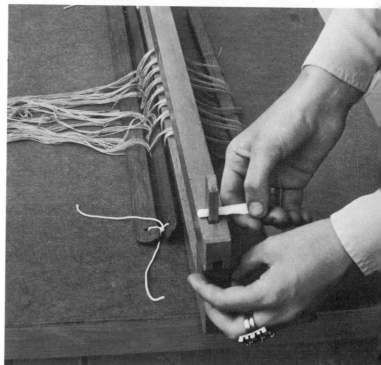

Fig. 3–12. The raddle tied to the back of the loom.

Figs. 3–13a, b and c. The back tie-up (below, and top and bottom right).

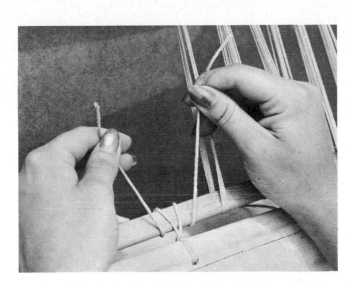

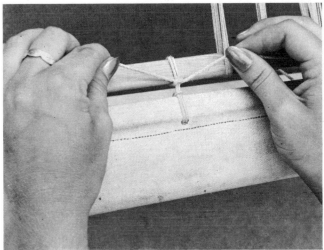

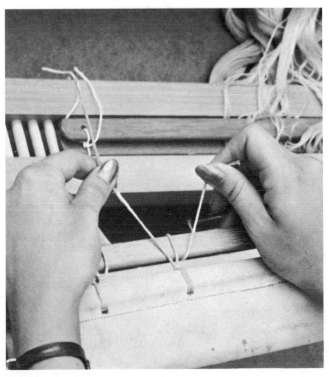

4. Setting Up the Loom

Beaming (Winding On the Warp)

YOUR WARP, tied to the warp beam, and still on the raddle, is now ready to be *beamed (rolled)* on to the warp beam.

Preparing Your Loom. *2-way loom:* to prepare for beaming, simply loosen the back wing screw of the roller.

4-shaft loom: push the *heddles* to the sides to allow the warp to pass through the middle and push the reed forward to rest on the front beam (Fig. 4–1). (If the warp stretches the full width of the reed, the shafts can be taken out from the grooves at the side of the loom for beaming.)

Make sure that the pawl is engaged in the teeth of the ratchet wheel at the back of the loom.

Rolling On with Two People. It is much easier to roll the warp on if you have someone to help you. While one person winds the warp on to the back beam, by turning the back

roller, the helper, standing centrally a few feet in front of the loom, holds the warp taut with both hands. As the warp runs smoothly through the raddle and the cross and on to the back roller the front helper gradually releases it from the chain (Fig. 4–1).

Start by rolling on the *apron* and, as soon as one complete turn of the roller has been made, cover the knots attaching the warp to the back roller with one or two warp sticks (Fig. A–8, Appendix A), otherwise the unevenness of these knots will cause bad tension. At each revolution of the roller use a warp stick (if sticks are not available feed in a piece of firm paper, cut the same width as the apron and with a hem of about 1 in. folded under at each side).

The front helper should pull on the warp at intervals to tighten it on the back roller, which is held firm by the ratchet and pawl on a 4-way loom. If you are using a 2-way loom, you should stop rolling every now and again and secure the back roller; then pull on the warp, otherwise it will slip when the front helper is pulling steadily on the

Fig. 4–1. Beaming or winding on.

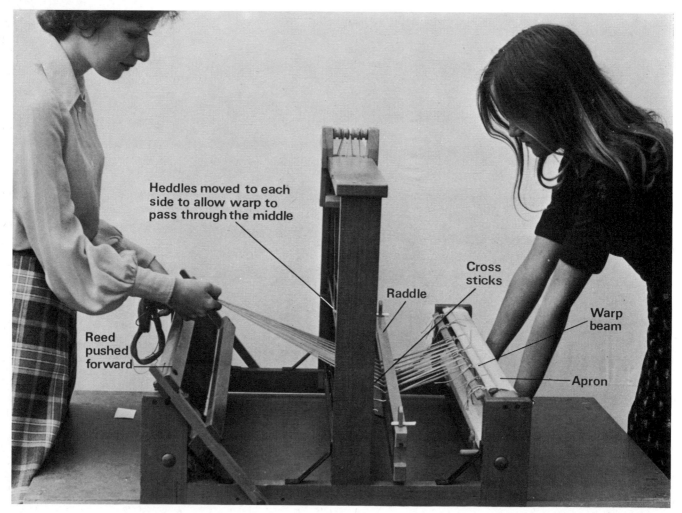

warp to tighten it. Then, grasping the warp sticks, pull them forward to allow more warp to run through the cross. Next, comb the raddle through the warp as far as it will come. Any warp ends which are tangled or loose may be straightened out by smoothing them forwards towards the unwinding chain of warp (Fig. 4–3); if you dampen your hands it will help at this stage. Roll on more warp, using warp sticks or paper between the layers of warp round the back roller. Repeat the process of winding on, tensioning and smoothing the threads, and remember that correct beaming will produce a firm back beam, with good tension on each warp end.

When only about 20 in. of warp remains, remove the raddle and cut through the warp ends at the loop so that the warp ends are ready for threading (Fig. 4–4).

Rolling On by Yourself. Roll on one turn at a time and secure the back beam. Then come to the front of the loom and pull the warp towards you, tightening it round the back beam. Smooth tangled threads to the front. If you are using a light loom it will need to be clamped to the table to keep it firm.

As this procedure is a lengthy one it is worth making the effort to enlist the services of a friend, if this can be arranged.

(For warping with two crosses and beaming the warp through the raddle, see Appendix A.)

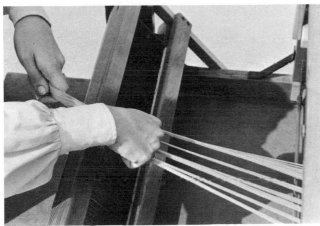

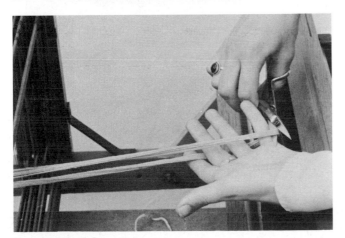

Fig. 4–2. Beaming or winding on the warp – the position of the hands on the back roller (top).

Fig. 4–3. Combing the warp with the fingers to smooth any tangled threads (above left).

Fig. 4–4. Cutting the warp loops (left).

27

Threading the Heddle (2-Way Loom)

The warp is now ready for threading and before starting the process you should undo the screws a little in the heddle clamp or holder, leaving a space between the two blocks of wood for the heddle. Place the heddle in this space in the clamp and tighten the screws. Put the clamp holding the heddle inside the loom on the table.

Now mark the middle of the heddle and the centre of the warp ends. Tie the warp sticks to the back of the loom in order to hold the warp steady. Before starting to thread, pull the centre-left section of the warp towards you with your left hand, and with your right-hand index finger move the threads along to the right, at the cross, noting the way in which they come through the space between the sticks. When this sequence is quite clear to you, you can start threading, taking the threads from over and then from under the nearer of the warp sticks.

First, lay the left section of the warp over the top of the heddle. Working from the middle to the left, take each thread of the warp through hole and space alternately, until you reach the end selvedge threads. These are put double through the heddle. Return to the middle of the warp and thread the other side (Fig. 4–5). Check each section of warp as you work, making sure that there is an end in every hole and space and double selvedge ends at each edge. Tie each section of about 12 ends in an overhand knot (Figs. 4–6 and 4–7), in front of the heddle.

Fig. 4–5. Threading a 2-way loom.

Fig. 4–6. Overhand knot. Make a ring with yarn. Pull a loop of yarn through the ring. Release the knot by pulling the loose end.

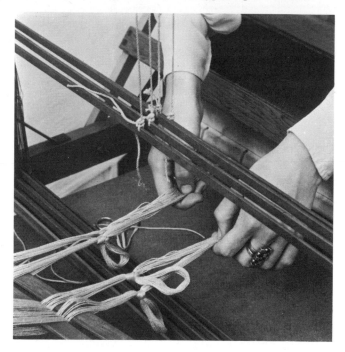

Fig. 4–7. Warp tied in overhand knots.

The Front Tie-Up. Check the threading right across the heddle and untie the string holding the shed sticks at the back of the loom. *Leave the shed sticks tied together at the cross sticks.* Loosen the front screw and roll up the apron until the warp stick held in it just comes over the top bar at the front of the loom. Tighten the front screw.

Tie another warp stick parallel to the one inside the apron seam, using the knot described in the back tie-up (see page 24, and Figs. 3–13a, b and c). Then undo the first overhand knot at the right of the warp. Pull this section of warp towards you and take it over the top of the warp stick you have just tied on and down between the two warp sticks. Divide it into two equal parts underneath and bring each half up again at each side and tie across the bunch of threads (Figs. 4–8a and b). Do the same at the other edge of the warp; this will support the heddle. Then tie the remaining warp in this way, working outwards from the centre. Tension each knot in this way (Fig. 4–8c). Pull the ends of the knots away from yourself and, holding that tension, make a second knot on top of the first (Fig. 4–8d). When both sets of knots are completed, run a finger across the bunches between the two knots to check that the tension is the same. Keep the ends of these knots as short as possible; wasted length at this stage will reduce your weaving length (remember that your allowance for wastage in front and back tie-up is only 15 in.).

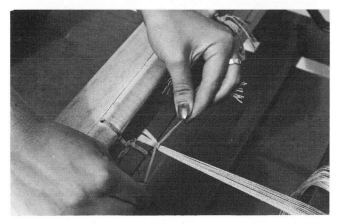

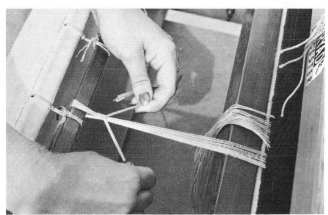

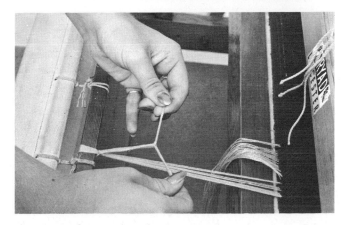

Fig. 4–8a. *The tie-up at the front of the loom. Making the first knot.*

Fig. 4–8b. *The first knot.*

Fig. 4–8c. *The tie-up at the front of the loom. Putting tension on the first knot.*

Fig. 4–8d. *The tie-up at the front of the loom. Making the second knot.*

Threading the Heddles and Reed (4-Shaft Loom)

The warp ends are threaded according to the *pattern draft* (a drawing of the pattern on squared paper, showing both threading and weaving order). Chapter 5 (see page 32) explains how to follow a pattern draft, and after reading through the threading instructions on the following pages you should study *Chapter 5* with close attention: you can then return to the threading instructions with a clear understanding of how to thread your warp according to a given pattern.

Weave Patterns. The most basic of weaves is the *plain* or *tabby* weave, which follows the same procedure as darning: this is the only weave possible on a 2-way loom. For your first piece of weaving on a 4-shaft loom, thread the loom with a straight draft, putting one warp end on each shaft in turn. This threading is called *straight threading* or *twill*, because twill patterns can be woven from it as well as plain cloth. It is the best weave for a beginner to use, since it is both simple and versatile.

Checking the Heddles. Before any threading takes place you should replace the shafts and reed, if they were removed for beaming. Check that there are enough *heddles* on each shaft for the draft. To do this, count the number of heddles needed on each shaft for one pattern and multiply by the number of patterns to be threaded (see page 28). Each doubled selvedge thread is treated as one and needs a heddle. Check that no heddles are crossed on the shafts, and leave a few spares at each side on the shafts.

Threading a 4-Shaft Loom. When threading, work from right to left and be careful not to take any threads out of order from the cross.

If you are using a *Harris* loom, arrange the heddles equally at each side of the central chain. If you are using a *Dryad* loom, untie the cords which attach the shafts to the pulleys. The grooves and blocks of wood on which the shafts rest will keep them upright. Leave a few spare heddles on the right of each shaft and push most of the remainder to the extreme left, leaving about a dozen in the middle of each shaft.

Threading the Twill Pattern. Taking the heddles from the group in the middle of each shaft start to thread, using a threading hook and following the pattern draft for *twill* (see page 43). Take the first 2 warp ends and thread them on to shaft 4, the third and fourth warp ends on to shaft 3, the fifth and sixth on to shaft 2 and the seventh and eighth on to shaft 1. This completes the right-hand selvedge. Then start threading singly on to 4321 (i.e. following the same routine), taking each shaft in turn, until the left-hand selvedge is reached. These last 4 heddles must be threaded double.

When threading, hold the warp thread taut over the

first two fingers of your left hand and down between the thumb and first finger. Then, with hook upward, pull on the taut part of the thread to bring it through the eye (Figs. 4–9 and 4–10).

Check each pattern as it is threaded and tie at the front of the heddles in an overhand knot (Fig. 4–6). Tie the warp ends in even groups.

The Reed. The function of the *reed* is to *beat the weft* and to act as a *spacer* to hold the warp ends at a certain distance from one another. The space depends on the *dent of the reed (number of slits to the inch)* and the number of ends put through each *dent (the spaces in a reed)*. For this first piece of weaving use a 14 dent reed, available with both Harris and Dryad looms, and place the warp ends singly in each dent of the reed (normally only coarse yarns – 4/2 or 6/2, equivalent to 3 or 4 ply wool – would be used in this way).

Fig. 4–9. Threading the heddles. Putting the thread on the hook and through the eye of the heddle.

Fig. 4–10. Threading the heddles. Pulling the thread through the eye of the heddle.

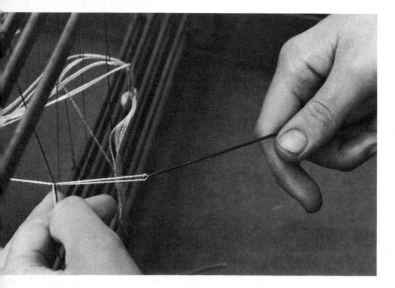

Threading the Reed. Mark the middle of the reed and of the warp. Untie the first bunch in the left-hand half of the warp and lay it over the top of the reed. Then, starting from the right, take the threads from this left-hand bunch, in order, and put them singly in each dent of the reed, using a flat reed hook (Figs. 4–11 and 4–12). Work until the left side is complete, taking double selvedge ends double through the reed. Then return to the middle and thread the right-hand side of the warp through the reed, working from left to right.

When reeding is completed, the warp ends should be in the same sequence at the cross, the heddles and the reed; the heddles should be in their correct place on the shafts, and the warp in line ready to tie up to the front of the loom. When tying up to the front follow the instructions given for a 2-way loom (see page 28, and Figs. 4–8a—d).

Slinging Heddle Frames or Shafts. The warp is now threaded on the loom. Check that each shaft is connected with the levers or buttons which are used to raise it, and that all the shafts are on the same level. On Harris looms make sure the chain on each shaft is central and correctly slung. For Dryad looms cut 4 lengths of fine loom cord about 30 in. long. Tie a large knot on one end of each length and thread with the large wooden shape provided (this is like a large, bell-shaped button). Take the other end of one of the strings and thread it upwards through the appropriate small hole in the top of the canopy, over the roller and down through the other two larger holes. Then thread the end through the central hole in the top horizontal

Fig. 4–11. Threading the reed. Finding the correct warp thread.

shaft bar and tie with a firm double knot. Finally, pull the wooden button down and engage it in the slit provided. That shaft should rise to form a shed. Repeat for the other 3 shafts (Fig. 4–13), making sure that no long ends of loom cord are hanging down at the warp level; they could break the warp ends when weaving commences.

Fig. 4–12. Threading the reed. Pulling the thread through the reed (below top).

Fig. 4–13. How to tie the shafts (below bottom).

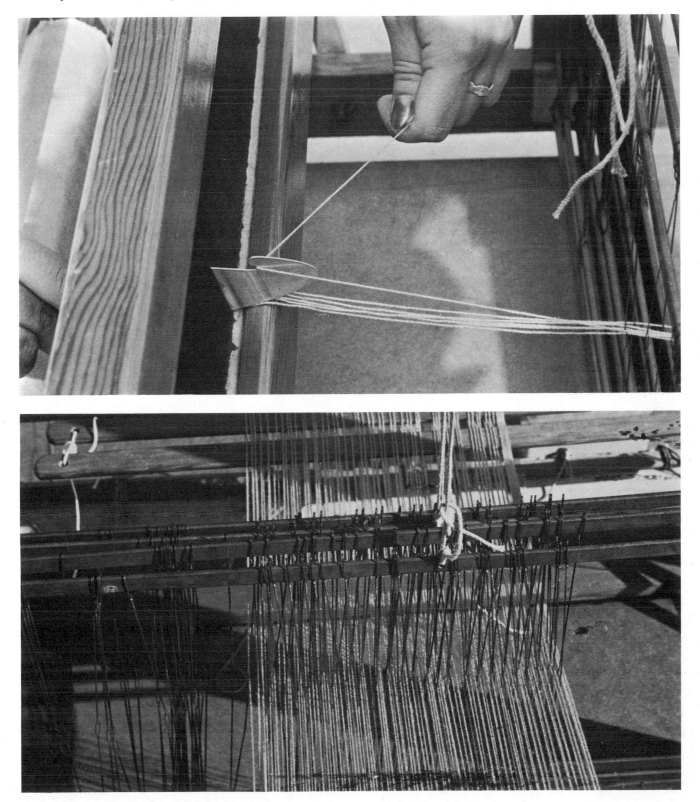

5. How to Use Pattern Drafts

A PATTERN DRAFT is a weaver's shorthand – *the diagram of a weave*. There are two parts to a full draft: the first part, the *threading plan,* shows how the warp ends are to be threaded through the heddles on the shafts (Fig. 5–1); the second part, the *weave plan,* follows directly below the threading plan and shows the order of intersection of warp and weft (Fig. 5–2). Beside the weave plan, the movement of shafts is shown for each *pick (row of weft).* (With treadle or foot power looms – see Appendix F – it is necessary to indicate on the draft how the shafts are tied to the pedals.)

There are many different ways of pattern drafting but they all have the above principles in common. The method described in this book is easy to follow, and has been selected for this reason.

Pattern drafts are written on point or squared paper, ¼ in. squares being a suitable choice. It is important to remember to read drafts from *right to left* as this is the order in which the pattern is threaded. Selvedges are omitted from the drafts and are dealt with separately (page 51).

There are few books which give drafts for table looms alone. The beginner, looking for weaves to use on a table loom, is often confused by details of tie-ups worked out for floor looms. As the scope of this book is limited to the table loom, unnecessary information has not been included.

Weave Plans

As most table looms operate with a rising shed the filled-in, black squares represent a warp thread up. Unfilled squares show warp threads down (covered by weft threads).

Drafting on a 2-Way Loom. Drafting on a 2-way loom is simple, since the loom allows only for plain weave.

Examine the two horizontal lines of squares on squared paper (Fig. 5–1); this is the *threading plan.* The squares marked 2 on the top row indicate that a warp end has been placed in a hole; the squares marked 1 on the bottom row show threads placed in spaces or slits.

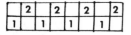

Threads placed in holes.
Threads placed in spaces.

Fig. 5–1. Two-way plain weave. Threading plan.

Row 1.
Row 2.

Fig. 5–2. Two-way plain weave. Weave intersection plan.

Next, examine the *weave intersection plan* (Fig. 5–2). This should be interpreted as follows:
Row 1: by raising the heddle all threads held in the holes (filled-in squares) will be raised.
Row 2: by depressing the heddle, all threads held in the holes (unfilled squares) will be lowered. It is the threads in the spaces which rise now; they are shown as filled-in squares on the draft in row 2.

Drafting on a 4-Shaft Loom. Drafting on a 4-shaft loom is rather more complicated, because there are several combinations of shafts which can form the shed.

A block of 4 horizontal squares is marked to represent the 4 shafts seen from above (Fig. 5–3). The bottom row represents shaft 1 (the shaft nearest the reed), the second and third rows represent the middle shafts, and the top row represents shaft 4, the back shaft (in other words, the one furthest from the weaver).

Back shaft (shaft 4)
Third shaft (shaft 3)
Second shaft (shaft 2)
Front shaft (shaft 1)

Fig. 5–3. Four ways to draft twill or straight threading.

Four Ways to Draft Twill or Straight Threading. The four diagrams in Fig. 5–3 show different ways of drafting the same *threading plan.* Along the horizontal rows of squares, those squares marked by a cross, a diagonal line, filled-in, or numbered, mean that a warp end has been placed in a heddle on that shaft. Remembering to read from right to left, it follows that the first warp end has been put on shaft 4, the second on shaft 3, the third on shaft 2 and the fourth on shaft 1. This completes the first twill pattern. It is usual to show one repeat of a pattern only, but as twill is such a short draft two repeats have been drafted (Fig. 5–4). For threading the twill pattern on your first piece of weaving repeat this order of threading until the warp is complete.

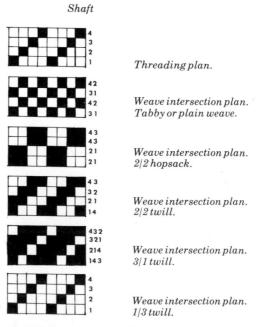

Shaft

Threading plan.

Weave intersection plan.
Tabby or plain weave.

Weave intersection plan.
2/2 hopsack.

Weave intersection plan.
2/2 twill.

Weave intersection plan.
3/1 twill.

Weave intersection plan.
1/3 twill.

Fig. 5–4. Weaves possible with twill: plain weave, 2/2 hopsack, 2/2 twill, 3/1 twill, 1/3 twill.

6. Selecting the Yarn and Filling the Shuttle

The Yarn

CHOOSE A YARN either the same thickness as the warp, or a little thicker. For the initial rows of weaving choose a contrasting colour, as this will make it easy to check mistakes in the weaving. After the initial rows have been woven you will be keen to experiment with other colours and textures. You can then examine and assess the inter-action of colours and yarns in the woven cloth.

Filling the Shuttle

Your first step will be to wind the weft yarns on to a bobbin, which is then inserted in a shuttle. You need a separate shuttle for each yarn. This process is known as *filling*.

The Simple Flat Shuttle. This is both the simplest and the cheapest type of shuttle, and the one used for most of the work illustrated in this book (Fig. 6–1a). Consisting of a flat piece of wood, with notches cut in each end to hold the yarn, it is filled by winding the yarn back and forth between the ends. The great advantage of this type of shuttle is that it is very simple to wind and to use, but it is slower than more sophisticated types of shuttle.

Fig. 6–1a. How to fill the simple flat shuttle.

Fig. 6–1b. How to fill the boat or roller shuttle.

The Boat or Roller Shuttle. This type of shuttle is quick to use, but both filling the bobbins and throwing the shuttle require practice. With this shuttle the yarn is held on a steel pin (Fig. 6–1b).

Filling the Bobbin. Bobbins are manufactured from wood, or can be home-made from stout brown paper or cartridge paper.

To make a paper bobbin, cut your paper into an oval shape slightly smaller than the space into which it will fit in the shuttle (Fig. 6–3). Roll the paper on the steel shaft of the bobbin winder and catch the end of the yarn in the last turn of the paper. Hold this end between the paper layers so that it does not slip, then wind a few turns by hand (Fig. 6–4). Now turn the handle in order to fill the

Fig. 6–2. The boat shuttle, yarn, paper bobbin or quill, and bobbin winder.

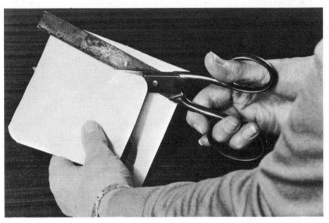

Fig. 6–3. Cutting the paper bobbin or quill for the shuttle.

Fig. 6–4. Starting to wind. The paper bobbin has been wrapped round the spindle of the winder.

33

D

bobbin, starting by building up a small mound of yarn at both ends, before filling the space in the middle (Figs. 6–5—6–7). Do this gradually until the bobbin is firm and well shaped, wide at the middle and evenly tapered at each end.

To fill a wooden bobbin, fasten the end of the yarn to the bobbin with adhesive tape, then wind evenly. Wind several spools at a time.

Fig. 6–5. Building up one end of the bobbin (below top).

Fig. 6–6. Shaping the other end (below middle).

Fig. 6–7. Shaping the middle (below bottom).

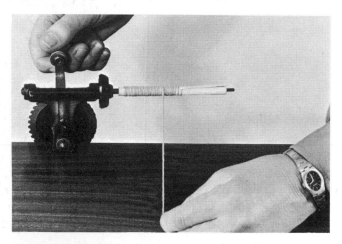

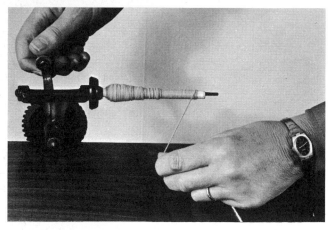

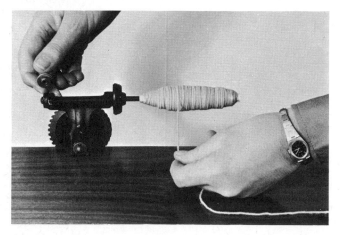

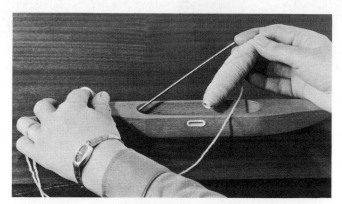

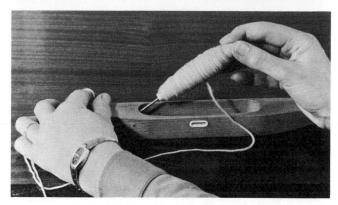

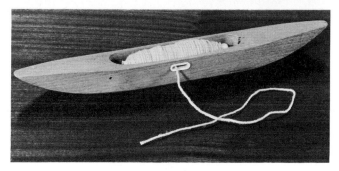

Fig. 6–8. The wound bobbin about to be put on the steel pin in the shuttle (above top).

Fig. 6–9. The bobbin on the pin (above middle).

Fig. 6–10. The filled shuttle (above bottom).

Inserting the Bobbin in the Shuttle. Put the bobbin in the shuttle so that the yarn runs from underneath, then pull the end through the hole and draw out a length ready for use (Figs. 6–8—6–10).

Using a Boat Shuttle

Practise with an empty shuttle first. Open the shed and, holding the shuttle with the index finger on its tip and your thumb on top, throw it to the other side of the warp with a flick of the index finger. Your other hand must be ready to catch the shuttle at the far side and return it (Fig. 6–11). With a hand-operated table loom the rhythm of using a boat shuttle can never be as smooth and continuous as on a foot power loom.

Fig. 6–11. Putting the shuttle in the shed.

7. Starting to Weave

Weaving on a 2-Way Loom

Now, AT LAST, you can start to weave! Your aim, to begin with, will be to learn to control the beater (heddle) so that the weaving is even, with equal amounts of warp and weft showing in the fabric. Try to keep a neat, straight edge, neither drawing the weft across too tightly, nor leaving weft loops at the edges.

Raise the heddle to bring up alternate warp threads, i.e. those held in the holes. The threads in the spaces or slits will sink to the bottom limit of the heddle. This action forms a triangular space, called a *shed* (Fig. 7–1), between the heddle and the front of the loom. Put a flat warp stick into this space, then make the opposite shed by pushing the heddle down firmly (Fig. 7–2). Insert another warp stick. This process draws the threads together, and fills up the spaces between the groups of warp threads tied to the front of the loom. Repeat the process, if necessary.

Raise the heddle and start to weave, inserting the filled shuttle and passing it through the shed from the right. Pull it out at the other side and pull the loose weft thread through until about an inch is left sticking out at the right selvedge.

Hold the heddle in the centre and beat it down towards you against this row of weaving, until it rests on the last warp stick. Push the heddle back. Take the end of the weft yarn and turn it round the end warp strand, bringing it back into the same row (heddle raised). This means that the first row of weaving will have a double thickness of weft yarn for an inch at the right edge. Change the shed by depressing the heddle, insert the shuttle from the left edge and weave the second row. Continue like this, alternating the two positions of the heddle to change the shed.

After you have woven a few inches, the *fell edge (the last row of weaving)* will be too near the heddle to make a good shed. Undo the back roller and let out a little more warp from the back beam. Then undo the front roller and wind on the cloth at the front until about 2 in. of weaving extends in front of the cloth beam (front roller). The cross or warp sticks will have moved with the warp, so return them to their correct position just over the top of the warp as it comes from the back beam. If they are left too near the heddle, they will stop the shed forming.

Joining Weft Yarns. Never join with a knot. To join fresh lengths of the same colour overlap the old and new weft yarn between a few warp ends (Fig. 7–3). This *splicing* should be carried out towards the edge, rather than in the middle of a row. If a thick yarn is used, splicing sometimes

Fig. 7–1. Two-way loom. Shed formed with heddle raised.

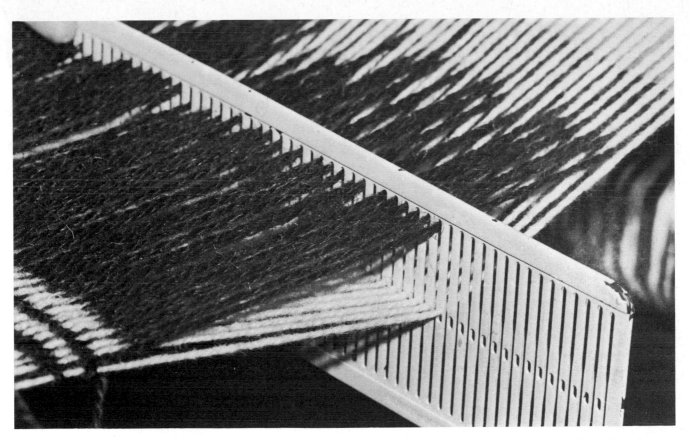

Fig. 7–2. Two-way loom. Shed formed with heddle lowered (above).

Fig. 7–3. Splicing. Joining in a new weft end without changing colour (below).

shows: if it does, cut off the old yarn at the selvedge, then use the new yarn, turning the end back into the same shed.

To join in a new colour, work as follows. Turn about 2 in. of the old colour into the same shed as the last row at the right selvedge. Introduce the shuttle with the new colour at the left selvedge and turn the end of the yarn back into the same shed as the first row of new colour at the left selvedge. When using two colours alternately, instead of cutting and joining at each row, carry the yarn up the selvedge like this. When both shuttles are out at the same selvedge, wrap the yarn on one around the yarn on the other to make a good edge, otherwise the edge threads will not be woven in on each row.

Experimenting. Even on a 2-way loom there are plenty of experiments you can carry out and plenty of different patterns you can try. Spanish lace, gauze, and warp or weft ovals are all easy to weave on 2-way looms. You can also experiment with free shuttle weaving and knotting, using thick and thin yarns *(all these techniques are described in Chapter 8).*

Experiment with colour. After you have used a contrasting yarn to enable mistakes to be seen easily, try a yarn of a similar colour to the warp – for instance a yellow warp with an orange weft. Then see what happens to the yellow warp when you weave with a pale blue weft. If your warp is rust coloured try a wine red yarn across it, then yellow, then black. You will learn by experience that the most difficult yarns to integrate are direct opposites in colour – orange woven with royal blue, emerald with flame, purple with yellow. These colours, because of the strength of contrast between them, do not blend well. They are better kept for deliberate contrast – in *multiple picks,* for example.

Fig. 7–4. Use of multiple picks. The thickest have 8 weft strands in the same pick.

A multiple pick (Fig. 7–4) is made by returning the weft thread into the same shed more than once before the shed is changed. Obviously it is necessary to take the weft thread round the end warp thread each time, otherwise the weft will just pull out. Multiple picks make flat, ribbon-like stripes in the weave.

By using a stick placed behind the heddle you can raise threads in groups by turning the stick on its edge.

Above all try different colours. It is exciting to see what happens when weft and warp mingle. You may want to make something to use from your first piece of cloth. In that case limit your experiments to the sample allowance. Then select what you are going to do and plan your piece of cloth to measure 20 in. × 9 in., which will make a bag to hold yarns, small shuttles etc. You could make a pattern using any of the experiments mentioned. (If you are weaving a repeating stripe pattern, measure the stripes, with tension released, before you roll on the cloth, to make both sides of the bag the same.)

Weaving on a 4-Shaft Loom

Your loom has been threaded in straight or twill pattern and you are in the fortunate position of being able to explore many weaves with this versatile threading.

Start by choosing a weft of similar thickness to the warp yarn, or a little thicker, and of a different colour. Concentrate on keeping a good edge and an even beat. If you require close-knit weft rows, beat once, then change the shed and beat once more before throwing the shuttle again.

Plain or Tabby Weave. Start your weaving with plain weave; for this you will need to study the draft for this weave (Fig. 5–4). Raise shafts 4 and 2 and insert a warp

stick in the shed formed in front of the reed (Fig. 7–5a). Bring the reed forward and use it to beat the stick into position at the front of the warp. Lower shafts 4 and 2. Raise shafts 3 and 1 and insert another warp stick in the shed, beating it down against the first stick (Fig. 7–5b). The use either of sticks, thick rug yarn or rags at the beginning of weaving helps to draw the warp together and close the V-shaped gaps between the groups of warp ends. Repeat, using two more sticks if necessary.

Fig. 7–5a. Four-shaft loom. Starting to weave. Inserting the sticks in the opposite sheds (below).

Fig. 7–5b. Inserting another warp stick in the shed (bottom).

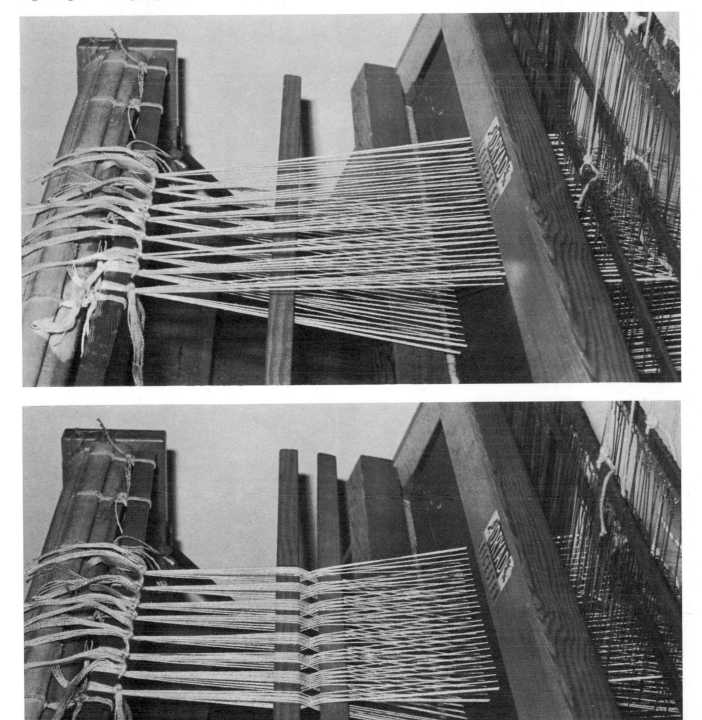

Fig. 7–6. *The first weft pick* (above).

Fig. 7–7. *Finishing off the end of the first pick of weft* (below).

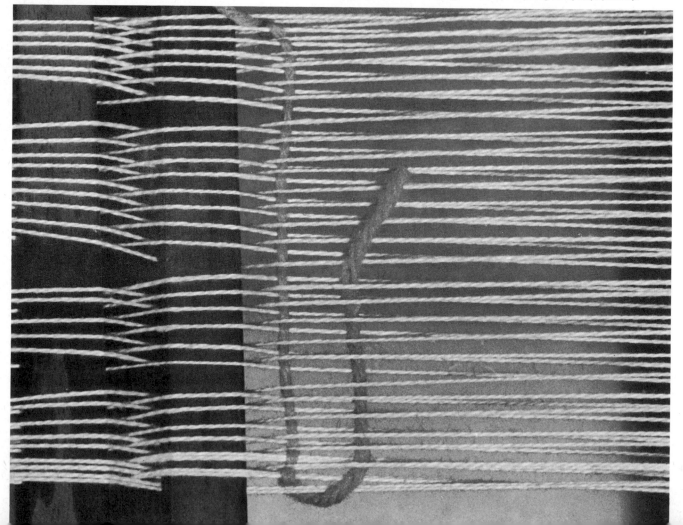

Raise 4 and 2 and with the right hand pass the filled shuttle through the shed from the right, leaving about 2 in. of weft yarn free from the warp at the right edge (Fig. 7–6). Take this weft end round the end warp thread and back into the same shed (Fig. 7–7). Beat this row or *pick* of weaving, so that it is pushed firmly against the edge of the last stick. Lower 4 and 2 and raise 3 and 1. Repeat the movement of the shuttle through the shed from left to right using your left hand.

Checking Your Weaving

There is a tendency, at the start, to pull the weft thread too tightly across the shed and so draw in the edge of the cloth. Weave about 1 in. and then check your work as follows:

(1) Is there an equal amount of warp and weft showing? If not, you are probably putting too much weight behind the beater instead of letting it beat with its own weight. Handle the beater in the middle.

(2) Are the edges neat and even? Loops on the edge of weft yarn mean that you are not pulling the weft tight enough. If, however, you are drawing in the edge too much, try holding the outside selvedge between the thumb and fingers of the hand which is not passing the shuttle. Leave an arc of weft yarn rising to about 4 in. in the shed before beating down.

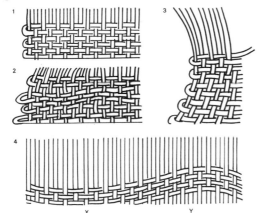

Fig. 7–8.
(1) An even woven edge.
(2) The weft has not been pulled in enough, causing loops of loose weft at the edge.
(3) Too tight a weft results in the edge pulling in.
(4) Uneven tension at the front tie-up. Adjust the front knots. Loosen at X. Tighten at Y.

(3) Is the row of weaving straight? If not, there is probably a fault at the front tie-up. Check that the sticks at the front, used in the tie-up, are parallel. Check the tension of the knots.

(4) Are there mistakes occurring in the actual weave? Check that the cords connecting shafts to pulleys are tight enough so that they will raise the shafts high enough to make a shed to pass the shuttle. It may be necessary to tighten the cloth roller a little. There may be an odd warp end which, because it is loose, is not rising properly in the shed. If so, trace this end to the front tie-up and re-tie this bunch, making sure that the slack thread is now as firm as the others. The slackness could also be caused by a very short warp end. In this case tie an extra length of yarn on to the short end to make tensioning easier.

(5) If a warp end breaks it is impossible to mend it by knotting the two ends together. Tie a long length of yarn on to the broken end at the back of the loom, using a weaver's knot because it is small, flat and will not slip under strain (Fig. 7–9). Then follow the track of the original end with the new length of yarn, bringing it forward, over and under the cross sticks, through the correct heddle and dent of the reed to the front of the loom. Place a dressmaker's pin in line with the broken end about an inch from the last row of weaving. Wind the new warp length round the pin in a figure eight and continue to weave using the new warp length. Undo the pin, which could cause damage, before you wind on that part of the cloth. When the work is finished you can undo the weaver's knot and darn all the ends in.

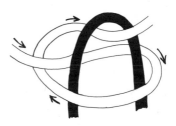

Fig. 7–9. The weaver's knot.

Finishing Cloth

Taking the Cloth off the Loom. When the first piece of cloth is completed, decide how you are going to finish the two fell edges. If you plan to overstitch or hem stitch the edges, stitch the back edge before you take the cloth off the loom. Alternatively the warp can be knotted in bunches close to the weaving. However, if this first piece of weaving is to be used solely as a sampler, finish both fell edges with a line of machine stitching.

To take the cloth off the loom, cut through the warp strands at the back of the loom. Pull the warp forward through the heddle on the 2-way loom, and off the heddles and reed on the 4-shaft loom. Untie the cloth at the front.

Washing Cloth. Cotton and linen are not difficult to finish. After washing in warm water, *cotton* should be ironed on the wrong side. If *fancy yarns* have been used, take care not to flatten the surface texture with heavy pressing. *Linen* should also be washed in warm water: this may have to be done several times, as the cloth often requires a number of pressings while still damp.

For information on *finishing wool*, which is rather more complicated, see Appendix A.

Records

Keep a simple record of all weaving done; such records are invaluable sources of reference when future projects are planned. For each piece of weaving note down the weight and colour of yarns used and the names of the relevant suppliers. It is also important to record the dent, pattern threading, number of picks per inch, measurements before and after finishing, and method of finishing. Also remember to note down any peculiarities of yarns used; some yarns behave and some don't. Only personal experience can teach you to choose yarns which will give the correct results for your requirements.

8. Weaves and Pattern Drafts

A. The Basic Weaves

Plain or Tabby Weave

(Fig. 5–4.)

A knowledge of plain weave is the foundation to the craft. In plain weave the warp and weft ends interlace singly as every other warp end is raised and one pick of weft is woven. It is the strongest weave because of this single interlacing, and so it is useful for any cloth which needs to be firm and durable. *Balanced plain weave* is cloth in which there are the same number of picks to warp ends in an inch, with warp and weft of equal thickness. *Weft rib cloth* is made by setting the warp ends wider (fewer ends to the inch) and beating the weft down hard to cover the warp ends. This is how *tapestry* is woven. The opposite type of cloth (a *warp rib*) is made by setting the warp close and using a thick weft yarn or a series of multiple picks.

Lacy patterns can be made in plain weave. In *gauze weave* (Fig. 8–23) the warp threads are twisted round one another. *Spanish lace* (Fig. 8–25) is woven by taking the weft yarn backwards and forwards in the sheds instead of straight across. Warp or weft threads can be tied or bunched together to make oval shapes in the cloth. Fine yarns and a planned spaced warp will enhance the lacy quality of these cloths.

A decorative effect on plain weave known as *soumak* can be made by wrapping the warp threads with the weft yarn in something like a stem stitch (Fig. 8–32). In between each row of soumak is a finer invisible plain pick. *Pile weaves* have yarns knotted on to the warp. *Free shuttle technique* (Fig. 8–34) consists of taking a thicker additional weft yarn in and out of the shed to make a pattern. Horizontal lines are made by the second weft resting in the shed, and vertical ones by passing the second weft under the finer ground weft at intervals.

All these cloths can be made on a simple 2-way loom with a rigid heddle.

Plain weave is also used as a basis for decorative cloths, where the pattern is made by long overshots or floats in the weft. In these patterns alternate sheds are woven in plain weave in a finer yarn than that used for the pattern picks. The plain weave is the binder and makes the cloth strong. With most pattern drafts, raising 4 and 2 and then 3 and 1 alternately makes plain weave. Using a binder, raise 4 and 2 and put the shuttle in from the right edge. Then, after the next pattern pick, raise 3 and 1 and weave with the shuttle going into the shed from the left. By observing this simple rule, you will always know, from the position of the shuttle, which tabby pick to use.

2/2 Hopsack

This is the best pattern to weave after plain weave, being, in effect, double tabby. In 2/2 hopsack the warp threads are raised in pairs and 2 picks of weft are woven before the shed is changed. The interlacing is in pairs (that is what 2/2 means), i.e. 2 shafts are raised and 2 are lowered.

(1) Raise 4 + 3, bringing up adjacent warp ends in pairs.
(2) Weave 2 picks without changing the shed. On the second pick the weft yarn must be taken round the end warp thread to lock it in the correct position. Do not pull in this second pick too much.
(3) Change the shed and raise 2 + 1.
(4) Weave 2 picks.

2/2 hopsack is softer to handle than plain weave. Because the distance between the warp ends is wider (as they are raised in pairs), the weft can be beaten down hard to make a close tapestry weave covering the warp completely. Thick and thin yarns alternating in the weft will result in ribbed cloth. (The pattern draft is in Fig. 5–4.)

Fig. 8–1. Cross check 2/2 twill.

Twills on a 4-Shaft Loom

There are three kinds of twill possible on a 4-shaft loom from a straight threading: 2/2, 3/1, and 1/3 twill.

2/2 Twill. (Figs. 5–4, 8–1 and 8–2.) This is a balanced weave like tabby and 2/2 hopsack, in that warp and weft intersect equally on each pick. This fabric is softer than plain weave and has more diagonal stretch. Both plain weave and 2/2 hopsack are formed by a straight substitution of warp threads up and warp threads down at the change of shed. 2/2 twill is formed by weft crossing over 2 warp ends moving sideways as each pick is woven, and forming a diagonal line on the cloth surface.

(1) Raise 4 + 3 and weave 1 pick.
(2) Raise 3 + 2 and weave 1 pick.
(3) Raise 2 + 1 and weave 1 pick.
(4) Raise 1 + 4 and weave 1 pick.
(5) Repeat these 4 picks.

Fig. 8–2.
A. *Dog tooth check. 2/2 twill.*
B. *Glen Urquhart. 2/2 twill.*
C. *Log cabin plain weave.*

3/1 and 1/3 Twills. (Fig. 5–4.) These are unbalanced weaves because the warp and weft do not divide equally. 3/1 twill is formed on the top surface of the cloth by raising 3 of the shafts together so that the weft only passes over 1 warp thread in 4. This is a *warp-faced cloth*. The reverse, a *weft-faced cloth*, is formed at the same time on the underside of the cloth, as more weft shows there.

(1) Raise 4 + 3 + 2 and weave 1 pick.
(2) Raise 3 + 2 + 1 and weave 1 pick.
(3) Raise 2 + 1 + 4 and weave 1 pick.
(4) Raise 1 + 4 + 3 and weave 1 pick.
(5) Repeat these 4 picks.

(N.B. Some purists insist that in clothmaking, as in tapestry, the top surface is the wrong side and the right side is the *underneath* of the cloth.)

To weave 1/3 twill on the top surface, raise single hed-dles on each shaft in turn.

(1) Raise 1 and weave 1 pick.
(2) Raise 4 and weave 1 pick.
(3) Raise 3 and weave 1 pick.
(4) Raise 2 and weave 1 pick.

The direction of twill line can be changed during weaving, giving *zig-zag patterns* of a vertical nature. For small zig-zags weave 7 picks, reversing the order on the fourth pick; weave 1 pick with the following shafts raised in turn: 4 + 3, 3 + 2, 2 + 1, 1 + 4, 2 + 1, 3 + 2, 4 + 3. The length of the zig-zags can vary, making wider zig-zags by weaving more picks in one direction before reversing the direc-

tion. They can be woven further in one direction than the other.

When weaving twills, the end warp thread does not always weave in with the cloth. Start the twill at the left selvedge and make sure that each weft row passes either under or over the end warp threads, making a firm edge.

Dog tooth, Glen Urquhart and log cabin are also twill patterns, but as they are *threaded in two colours* they are all dealt with under *Stripes and Checks* on page 58.

Pattern drafts have already been explained in Chapter 5 (see page 32). Briefly, a pattern draft is a *diagrammatical representation of a weave*. The following pages contain pattern drafts, as well as instructions, for a number of weaves and variations.

The commas between the groups of numbers in the instructions indicate that the groups are raised in turn: e.g. the instructions for herringbone would read as follows: raise shafts 43, 32, 21, 14. This means that for pick 1 you raise shafts 4 and 3, for pick 2 shafts 3 and 2, for pick 3 shafts 2 and 1, and for pick 4 shafts 1 and 4.

In some patterns, weaves can be made using a greater variety of combinations of shafts than appear on the examples shown in this book.

Tabby is usually woven by raising shafts 1 and 3, then 2 and 4, in turn. Any *exceptions in tabby shafts* are shown on the drafts.

Variations on twill weave are made by reversing the direction of the twill when threading the heddles. When woven as twill, horizontal *chevrons* appear on the cloth instead of diagonal lines. By reversing the twill in the weaving, *diamonds* are formed instead of vertical zig-zags.

Point twill, *goose eye* and *herringbone* can be woven without a *binder*. Rosepath is generally used as a pattern stripe in thick yarn with a binder yarn in tabby in between each pattern pick. In *herringbone*, raising shafts 1 and 3, and then 2 and 4, will not give pure tabby; some warp ends will rise together in the weave. This is because there are odd, or even, adjacent ends in the pattern threading. In the other twills, threads occur alternately on odd and even shafts.

Shaft

Fig. 8–3.
Threading plan. Point twill.

Point Twill

Pattern draft Fig. 8–3 (encircled thread on final pattern only).
Tabby
Raise shafts in this order:
42, 13, as with twill.
Diamond all over pattern (thin line)
Raise 4, 3, 2, 1, 2, 3
Finally add 4 to balance pattern.
Diamond all over pattern (thicker line)
Raise 43, 32, 21, 14, 21, 32
Finally add 43 to balance pattern.
Diamond stripes
Raise 43, 32, 21, 14, 21, 32, 43
Use tabby in between stripes. To lengthen the centre raise

14 several times and use a binder row in tabby in between each pattern pick.

A bolder pattern is woven by the following shaft positions. This should have a binder yarn used throughout: 41, ×2 (i.e. 2 picks), 43, ×3, 23, ×2, 12, ×4, 23, ×2, 43, ×3, 41, ×2.

Rosepath

(Fig. 8–5.)
Pattern draft Fig. 8–4.
All over pattern
Raise shafts 43, 32, 21, 14, 12, 32
Repeat this sequence of picks, adding 43 finally to balance pattern.
Stripe pattern
Raise shafts 43, 32, 21 (1 pick each)
Raise shafts 14 and weave 7 picks using a tabby binder between each pattern pick, then reverse the pattern, weaving 1 pick each of 21, 32 and 43 to balance the pattern. Use tabby weave between stripes.
Alternative pattern
Raise shafts 12, ×2 (i.e. 2 picks), 41, ×2, 34, ×2, 23, ×4, 34, ×2, 41, ×2, 12, ×2.
Use a tabby binder between each pattern.

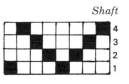

Shaft

Fig. 8–4.
Threading plan. Rosepath.

Fig. 8–5. Rosepath in plastic raffia. 2/4 cotton warp (opposite).

Goose Eye

(Figs. 8–7, 8–8 and 8–9.)
Pattern draft Fig. 8–6 (encircled thread on final pattern only).
Diamond pattern
Raise shafts 23, 34, 14, 12, 23, 34, 14, 12, 23, 34, 14, 34, 23, 12, 14, 34, 23, 12, 14, 34, 23, 12
Repeat this sequence.
Herringbone-type pattern (chevrons running in horizontal lines across the cloth)
Raise shafts 41, 43, 32, 12, and repeat.

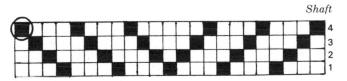

Shaft

Fig. 8–6.
Threading plan. Goose eye.

Fig. 8–7. Book cover, goose eye (top right).

Fig. 8–8. Goose eye (below right).

Fig. 8–9. Bag in fine cotton, goose eye. Macramé handle (overleaf).

Herringbone

(Fig. 8–10.)
Pattern draft Fig. 8–11
Herringbone
Raise shafts 43, 32, 21, 14, and repeat.
Diamond all over pattern
43, 32, 21, 14, 21, 32, 43

Fig. 8–10. Herringbone (below top).

Fig. 8–11.
Threading plan. Herringbone.

Fig. 8–12. Herringbone draft. Shafts raised. 4 + 3, 3 + 2, 2 + 1, 1 + 4 and repeat (below bottom).

Waffle

(Fig. 8–13.)

This weave is another variation of twill, the reverse points in the pattern being emphasized by the way it is woven. The cloth is made with long floats of warp on the right and left of a square with weft floats at top and bottom. The pockets of plain cloth inside the square are not as deep when woven on 4 shafts as when they are woven on 8 shafts. *Denting* should be close, 20—28 depending on the thickness of the yarn. Wools or soft cottons are recommended. The weave draws in more than in twill, so extra warp width allowance must be made. The weft should be either the same thickness as the warp, or a little thicker.

Pattern draft Fig. 8–14 (encircled thread on final pattern only).

Weaving waffle

Raise 432, 431, 42, 3, 4, 3, 42, 431

This sequence of picks forms the pattern. Finally, add 432 to balance the pattern.

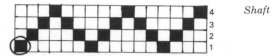

Shaft

Fig. 8–14.
Threading plan. Waffle.

Fig. 8–13. Heavy curtaining, waffle (below).

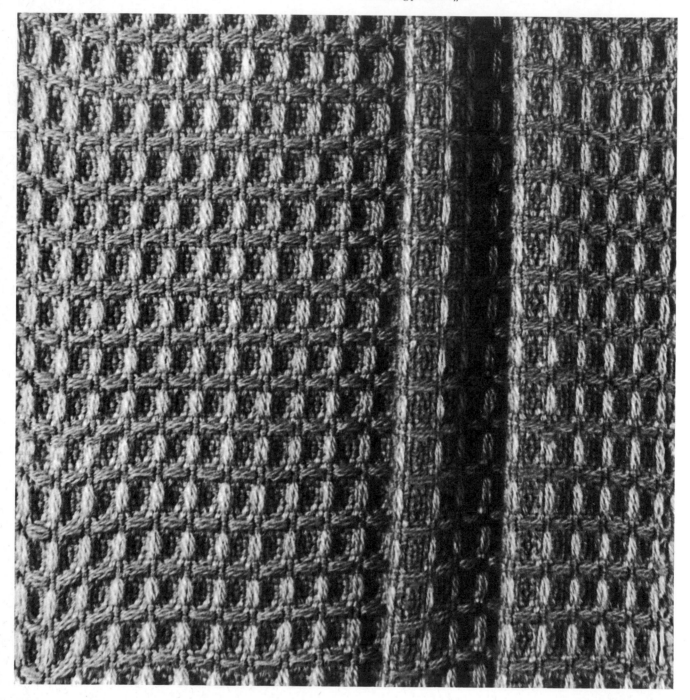

Fig. 8–15. Handbag with macramé handle. Summer and winter weave. Warp is threaded in blocks of 8, 12 and 16 ends in two colours.

Summer and Winter Weave

(Fig. 8–15.)
This is a clear-cut pattern and, as no overshot thread goes over more than 3 ends, it is suitable for a wider variety of cloths than other decorative patterns. Every other warp thread is entered on 1 or 2 shafts. These are the binding down threads; the patterns are formed by the other shafts. The cloth, which is equally suitable for fine and coarse yarns, has more weft on one side and more warp showing on the other. The two blocks consist of 4 warp ends each. They are:
Block A: 4241
Block B: 3231
How many times the blocks are used can be varied, as shown in the draft. Colour change can be used across the warp, or one colour used throughout. Tabby is formed on 4 and 3 and 1 and 2 alternately. If you use a binder you will weave a different cloth from one woven without a binder.
Pattern draft Fig. 8–16.
Weaving summer and winter weave
Raise shafts 13, 23, 14, 24 for 4 picks each, and repeat.
Tabby binder on shafts 12 and 34 between each pick.

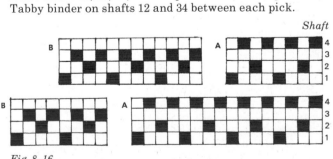

Shaft

Fig. 8–16.
Threading plan.
Summer and winter weave.

E

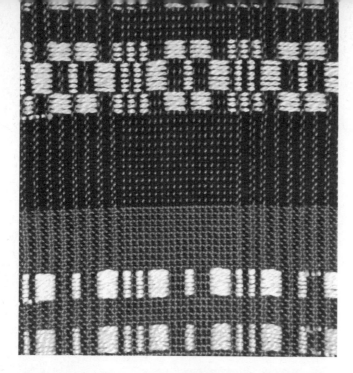

Monksbelt

(Figs. 8–17 and 8–18.)

Monksbelt is a decorative pattern on opposite blocks. Because of long floats or overshots of yarn forming on the surface, a thinner binder yarn is woven in tabby between the pattern picks. This is a bold pattern which can be used as a decorative stripe in a variety of ways.

Pattern draft Fig. 8–19.

Weaving monksbelt

Raise shafts 34, ×4, 12, ×6, 34, ×4

Fig. 8–17. Monksbelt (left).

Shaft

Fig. 8–19.
Threading plan. Monksbelt.

Fig. 8–18. Smocks with monksbelt yokes. This also shows the loom with shaft 2 raised to form a shed (below).

Honeysuckle

When warping, add an extra 7 ends to balance the pattern. These are threaded after the final pattern on shafts 1414141.

Pattern draft Fig. 8–20.

Weaving honeysuckle

Raise shafts 23, ×2, 34, ×2, 14, ×2, 12, ×2, 23, ×2, 12, ×2, 14, ×2, 34, ×2, 23, ×3

Alternative smaller pattern

Raise shafts 23, 34, 14, 12, 12, 14, 34, 23

Another alternative pattern

Raise shafts 23, 34, 41, 12.

These 4 picks in order 3 times.

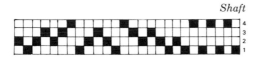

Shaft

Fig. 8–20.
Threading plan. Honeysuckle.

Swedish Lace

(Fig. 8–21.)

Lace weaves, as well as being finger manipulated, can be woven by using a particular pattern threaded on the heddles. These laces are not as delicate and individual as gauze because the pattern blocks are regular, forming small window-like patches of lace on a plain weave ground.

Fig. 8–21. Swedish lace in two colours.

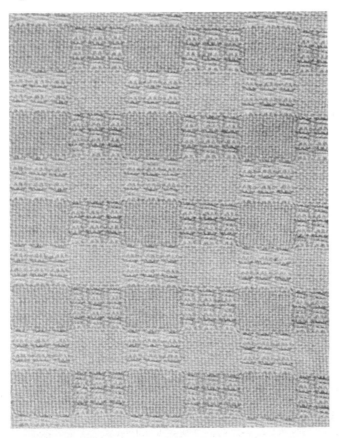

Pattern draft Fig. 8–22.

Weaving Swedish lace

Raise shafts 24, 123, 24, 123, 24 ⎫
                              13,
         24, 123, 24, 123, 24 ⎬ Block A
                              13,
         24, 123, 24, 123, 24 ⎭

         13, 234, 13, 234, 13 ⎫
                              24,
         13, 234, 13, 234, 13 ⎬ Block B
                              24,
         13, 234, 13, 234, 13 ⎭

The size of the blocks can vary. By repeating one block only, the cloth will consist of vertical lace stripes.

Shaft

Fig. 8–22.
Threading plan. Swedish lace.

Selvedges

Selvedge ends are doubled for extra strength and threaded in twill or plain weave. Write out the pattern on squared paper, and you will then be able to see the direction in which the selvedge should be threaded and whether any extra threads are needed to balance the pattern, i.e. to make both edges of the cloth the same.

Example: Rosepath (Fig. 8–4). In this pattern either add 7 ends after the last pattern and thread 4321, 234, or omit the final end of the last pattern which is threaded on 1. This balances the pattern. Then add the selvedge ends, drawing them on the draft. The right selvedge should be threaded 4321 and the left selvedge 1234. The direction of the selvedges will follow the same line as the pattern.

Four doubled selvedge ends at each side are enough for most cloths. Allow 2 extra ends only for narrow widths.

With fine yarns, instead of threading both heddles and reed double, thread selvedge ends singly through the heddles and double them at the reed.

B. Variations on Basic Weaves

Gauze Weave or Leno

(Figs. 8–23 and 8–24.)
This is a very old pattern. In Pre-Columbian Peru the most beautiful work was done in this technique on primitive looms. Treasured items in museums show an unsurpassed delicacy and understanding of materials.

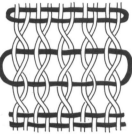

Fig. 8–23. Gauze weave.

Gauze can be made on a 2-way loom, the twisted pick being made with the heddle down. It is worked from right to left.

(1) Weave in plain for about 2 in.
(2) Slacken tension on the loom slightly. Use a pointed stick or a knitting pin to make the twisted pick. Start from the right and, with the shed opened for plain weave, take the first 2 threads from the bottom on the stick and over the top 2 threads, thus twisting them round each other. Keep them on the stick, pick up the next 2 and twist them over the top 2. When you reach the end of the pick, insert the shuttle in the space opened by the pick up stick turned on its edge, and pull the yarn through.

Fig. 8–24. Detail of gauze (below).

(3) Beat.
(4) Change the shed, beat hard, and then weave in the usual way. This row will hold the twist in place.
(5) Work these 2 picks in order. Threads may be twisted singly, in pairs, or in even multiples of warp ends.

This is finger manipulated gauze, as opposed to Swedish lace (Fig. 8–21), which is made by threading a pattern on the heddles.

Spanish Lace

(Figs. 8–25 and 8–26. Colour plate 13.)
This is another old technique.

(1) Weave 2 in. of plain weave.
(2) Decide how wide your blocks of lace weave are to be. If you want to have 3 blocks of lace in the cloth take your shuttle from the right to the end of the first block, or across one-third of the total width. Bring the shuttle out of the shed. Beat with the tip of the shuttle.
(3) Change the shed and return the shuttle to the right selvedge. Beat.
(4) Change the shed and weave one-third again. Beat.
(5) Change the shed and return the shuttle to the right selvedge. Beat.
(6) Change the shed and this time weave to the next group, i.e. two-thirds of the way across the warp. Beat.
(7) Weave on this group of threads the same number of picks as the first third. Beat.
(8) Carry the weft across to the left selvedge and weave the same number of picks across this last group. Beat.

Fig. 8–25. Spanish lace.

Fig. 8–26. Detail of Spanish lace (opposite).

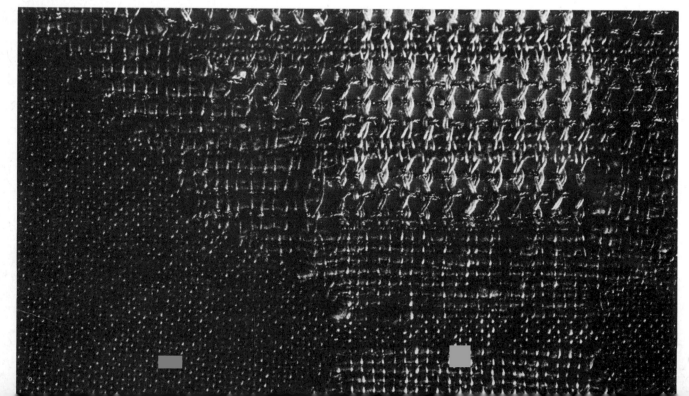

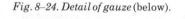

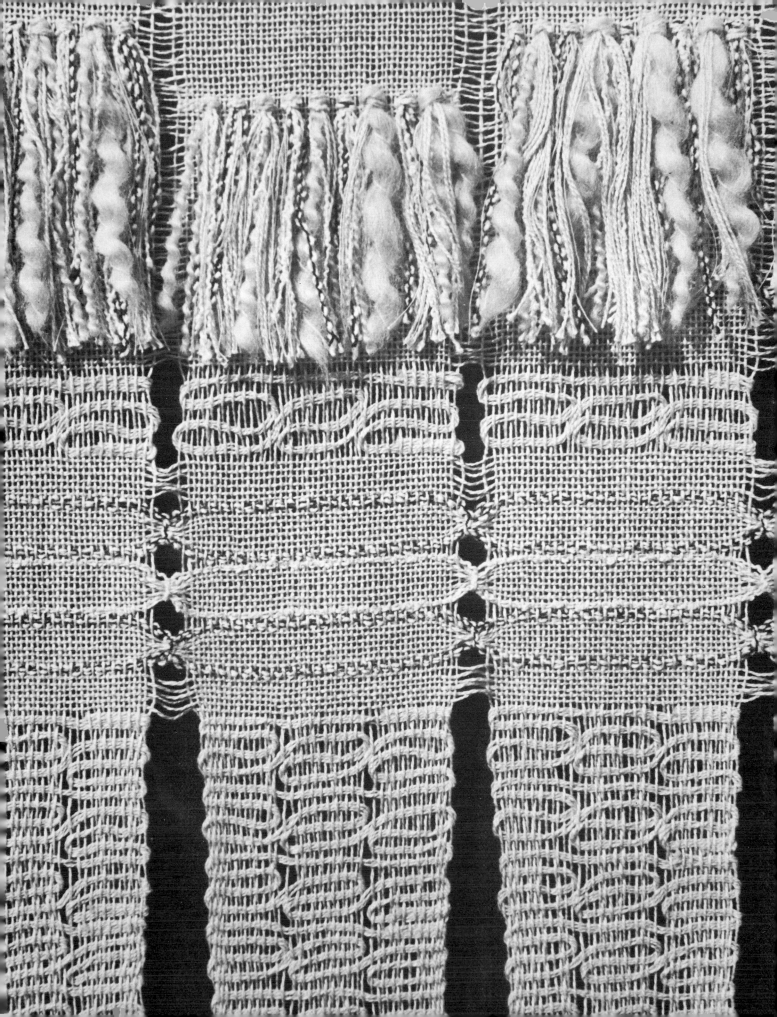

Grouping of Warp Ends to Make Lace

(1) Weave 2 in. in plain weave, finishing on the right.

(2) Decide how wide your oval patterns are to be, i.e. how many warp threads are to be grouped together (e.g. 5 ends in each group). Open the shed.

(3) Working from right to left, weave until you reach the place planned to start the first pattern. Then bring the shuttle out of the shed.

(4) Take the shuttle back over the last 5 warp ends and underneath them, bringing the shuttle through the loop formed.

(5) Weave to the end of the next 5 warp ends, than make a loop round these warp ends with the weft thread out of the shed.

(6) Continue until the planned pattern is complete, then weave to the edge.

(7) Change the shed and weave an uneven number of weft picks. This number depends upon how long you want the oval shapes to be. Then, starting from the right, repeat the whole sequence.

This pattern can be used for fine yarns on a *spaced warp* (Fig. 8–27) and is very suitable for curtains or lampshades, through which light needs to filter. In embroidery panels it will allow the background material to show. It can be combined successfully with the next pattern.

Fig. 8–27. Lampshade material on a spaced warp.

Grouping of Weft Threads to Make Lace

(Figs. 8–28 and 8–29. Colour plate 3.)
This is one of the simplest ways to create a lacy fabric. It is easiest to work on a spaced warp, but it can be woven with a normal denting.

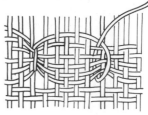

Fig. 8–28. Grouping of weft threads to make lace.

(1) Weave 2 in. in plain weave, finishing at the left selvedge.

(2) Decide how deep your oval patterns are to be, i.e. how many picks of weft you plan to draw up (e.g. 10 picks). It is easier to draw up the weft with the yarn off the shuttle, so cut off about three times the width of the warp from the yarn on the shuttle.

(3) Change the shed, and use your fingers to bring this weft yarn through the shed to the first space in the warp.

(4) Make a loop with the yarn and take it through the web from top to bottom below 10 picks of weaving. Pass it vertically under these 10 picks of weft and bring it up on to

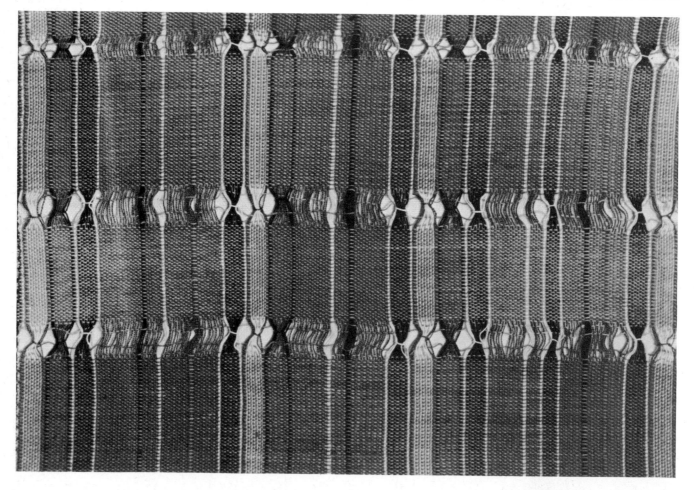

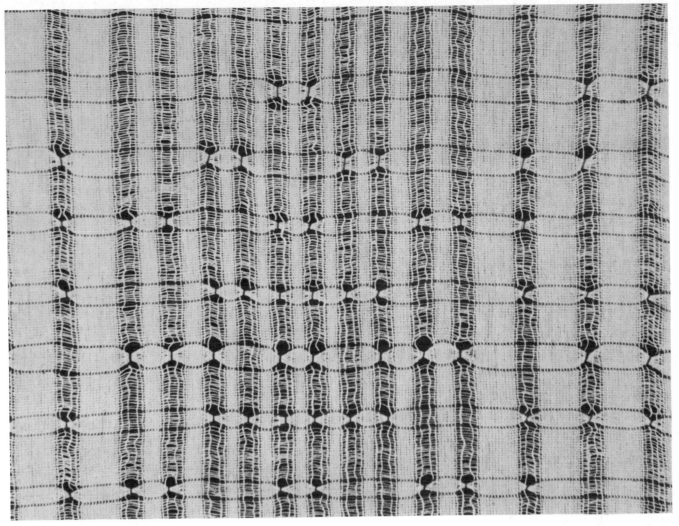

Fig. 8–29. Stole end, made on a spaced warp with lace ovals.

the top surface of the web in front of the pick you are weaving, so that it makes a loop.

(5) Take the weft thread through the shed to the next space and repeat the sequence until the right selvedge is reached.

This pattern can be used with one weight and colour of yarn. For the drawing up yarn, a heavier, contrasting yarn can be used, and more precise outlining of the shape can be made by weaving 2 picks in the same contrasting yarn before the 10 ground colour picks are woven. The drawing up is then done with the second pick of the next pair of contrasting yarn.

Oval sequins or stiff oval shapes in leather or acetate backed by thin white card can be introduced in hangings. When using these, weave until the sequin is reached in the shed and then pass the shuttle right underneath it and back into the shed for the next passage of plain weave, then underneath for the next sequin, and so on. Drawing up the ovals is done in the same way.

Knotted Pile on Plain Weave

(Fig. 8–31. Colour plates 4 and 7.)
Knots can be used to make a deep fringe, or as a pattern

within the design on the cloth. The density of the pile is determined by the number of knots per inch and the amount and type of yarn used. For wall hangings, where passages of encrusted surface are planned, knots can be invaluable. The length of pile can be uniform or can vary, and so can the yarn used. The length of the pile can be left undisturbed, or bound at intervals using a wrapping technique. In some you can pull the unbound lengths out: they will balloon out in varying ways depending on the yarn's character.

The simplest knot to use is a Ghiordes, a knot used in Turkish carpets (Fig. 8–30).

Fig. 8–30. Ghiordes knot.

(1) Weave about an inch in plain weave.
(2) Lay the lengths of cut yarn over 2 warp ends, taking the ends behind and between the 2, bringing them to the surface, beneath the yarn, over the 2 ends.

Fig. 8–31. Detail of fringe.

Soumak

(Figs. 8–32 and 8–33.)

This is a rug technique which can also be used in thinner cloth. It is similar to a stem stitch in embroidery and is worked with the weft yarn over the warp.

(1) Weave about an inch in plain weave.

(2) *Close the shed.* Using a thick yarn, take it over 2 warp ends and then round again. Leave the end of the weft hanging; it can be darned in later. Then continue across the cloth taking the yarn forward over 4 to the right and back under 2 *to the left* until the edge is reached, cutting the yarn after each row and darning the end in.

(3) Open the shed for the next correct tabby row and weave with finer binder yarn. Repeat the soumak from the left.

Soumak can be used to outline shapes, to give more definition to colour changes or to build up solid blocks of colour. Sisal, plastic strips or lengths of cloth can result in heavy surface texture. The binder yarn will not be seen if the entire surface is worked in soumak.

If the rows of soumak alternate from left and right, the lines of soumak will slant toward one another. Worked in one direction only, the lines will always move in that direction.

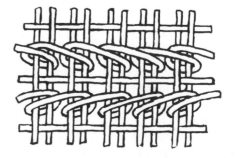

Fig. 8–32. Soumak technique.

Fig. 8–33. The use of soumak in clothmaking. Here, soumak is worked both ways alternately. This shows the slanting line of the yarn in opposite directions, similar to a knitted fabric. This piece of soumak is worked in unspun nylon sliver on a fine cotton warp, with a binder thread in the same fine cotton for alternate plain picks.

Free Shuttle Weaving

(Figs. 8–34 and 8–35.)
This technique is also known as *laid in weaving*, or *inlay*. Two wefts are used: one forms the cloth while the other, a thicker yarn, forms the laid in pattern. Both cloth and pattern can be woven in plain weave on a simple loom. Using a 4-shaft loom raise 1 shaft only for the pattern yarn. This will allow it to show more. Use normal plain weave for the background, i.e. the cloth. The horizontal lines are made simply by laying the pattern yarn in the shed. Vertical lines are made by passing the pattern yarn under the normal weft yarn used for the cloth, every fourth pick.

Fig. 8–34. Free shuttle inlay on a cushion cover. Made on a 2-way loom.

The ends of pattern weft can be cut and left on the top surface or taken as floats across the back. Simple square patterns in this technique can be useful for cushion covers. Unspun fleece can be used instead of thick yarn. More complicated shapes should be worked out on squared paper.

Fig. 8–35. Curtaining using free shuttle inlay in hourglass shapes.

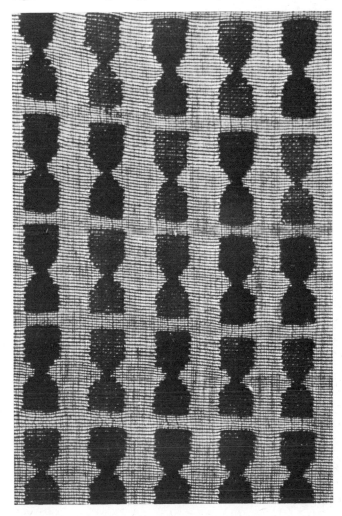

Stripes and Checks

Even Stripes and Checks. Horizontal stripes can easily be made in cloth by changes of colour in the weft. Textured fancy yarns or plain yarns may be used.

Vertical stripes have to be planned when making the warp. The stripes may be regular, for instance in 2 in. bands of contrasting colour, and woven with the weft thread matching one of the colours; alternatively, a completely different yarn can be used for the weft stripes.

Checked material is made by crossing even bands of colour with equal bands of the same colours in the weft. A variation of this is a pattern of 2 in. squares in the background framed by pairs in a contrasting colour. The background could be two or three different colours, or slight variations of one colour. The cross checks could alternate in colour or be all in one shade picked to contrast with the background squares.

Very narrow bands of warp and weft stripes will give tiny checks. A reversible twill check (dog tooth check) is made by 4 warp and 4 weft strands in two contrasting colours crossing one another in 2/2 twill (Figs. 8–2 and 8–36).

Glen Urquhart. (Fig. 8–2.) Glen Urquhart is a distinct check combining two blocks in warp and weft. One block is composed of 2 ends of two contrasting colours used alternately, the other consists of 4 ends of the same two colours. When woven in 2/2 twill this makes a cloth of small and larger checks.

Fig. 8–36. Reversible twill check, dog tooth.

Uneven Stripes and Checks. Very lively cloth can be made by striping the warp in varied colours and widths. This needs careful planning and you will have to decide whether to make your striping haphazard or symmetrical. Tone must be considered as well as colour. For example, thin pin stripes in yellow and white would show very strongly on a dark blue background, while black, purple, brown and dark red stripes would tend to merge into one another. Warping in every conceivable shade of red from geranium to magenta, combined with a bright pink weft yarn, will produce a totally dissimilar effect from a warp of pale tones of natural, beige and pink crossed with a white weft.

Tartan material is made by having the same successions of colours and widths of stripes in warp and weft. There are hundreds of different tartans to try, the colours most generally used being red, yellow, black, white, and light and dark blues and greens. All tartans, to be correct, must be woven in twill and the *sett* (i.e. the arrangement of threads) is prescribed. The wider blocks of threads forming the squares may be altered to fit the article to be woven. A 4-shaft loom capable of twill weave is needed to make a genuine tartan, but many interesting cross checks are possible on a 2-way loom (Colour plate 6).

Log Cabin Pattern. (Figs. 8–2 and 8–37.) Individual warp and weft threads in dark and light colours, woven in plain weave, result in a cloth which looks more intricate than it is! Use two contrasting colours (e.g. black and white) tied together to make the warp on a 4-shaft loom. Thread black and then white alternately through the heddles, black on 4, white on 3, black on 2 and white on 1. On a 2-way loom,

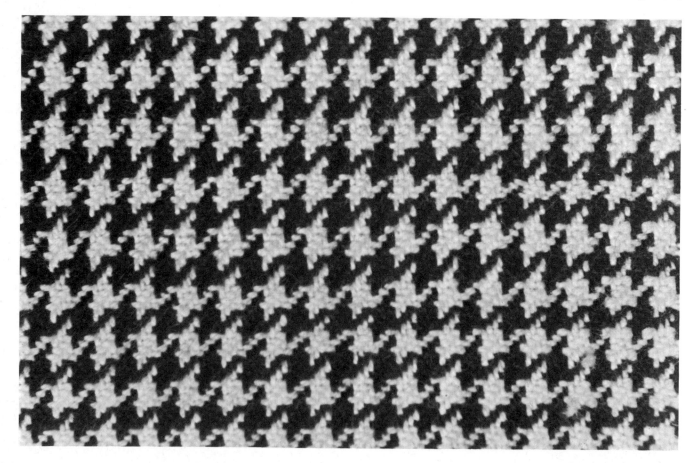

thread black in a hole and white in a space. Continue until all the threads in the first block are threaded. Then continue by threading the next block, taking the threads in the opposite order: white on 4, black on 3, white on 2 and black on 1. On a 2-way loom, white will be entered in a hole and black in a space. At the end of one block and the start of the next, 2 threads, either black or white will be adjacent. The blocks can vary in size but all this must be planned before starting to make the warp.

When the warp divides to make the shed, the black and white warp ends will rise in blocks, and if the weaving is done in black and white weft yarns, small motifs of horizontal and vertical pin stripes will form blocks which look rather like the individual logs in log cabin walls.

bone, for example. Use a suitable denting for the warp yarn chosen, to make a fairly firm cloth; the denting depends upon the reed on the loom. Don't make the sections too small. If necessary leave out 3 ends of each colour (fourth section).

Use the same yarns for the weft and follow the colour arrangement in the warp as a weave plan, using plain weave and twills. Try as many weaves as your warp length allows, not forgetting to reverse the direction of twill in the weave. You will be amazed at the variety of patterns that are possible. When you have finished the cloth, either cut it up, mounting and labelling the separate squares, or keep it in the length as a sampler.

A Colour and Weave Sampler

A practical way to study the structure of cloth is to make a colour and weave sampler. Choose two colours with a strong contrast in tone in a fairly coarse 2/4 cotton yarn; 4 ply wool and 9 and 11 cut tweed are also suitable. Plan to divide the warp into as many sections of 4 in. as you can; e.g. on a 24 in. wide reed 6 sections would be warped as follows: *first section* – use colour A alone; *second section* – 1 end colour A and 1 end colour B; *third section* – 2 ends colour A and colour B; *fourth section* – 3 ends colour A and colour B; *fifth section* – 4 ends colour A and colour B. All these sections will be in twill threading. Include one final section in colour B in one of the point twills: herring-

Fig. 8–37. Log cabin (a form of plain weave).

9. Tapestry

(Colour plates 8 and 17.)

VARIOUS KINDS OF EMBROIDERY are often incorrectly called tapestry. The Bayeux Tapestry is in fact an embroidered hanging showing in lively pictures the story of the Norman Conquest of England in 1066. Modern canvas embroidery – stitchery worked on fine or coarse canvas with wool or silk – is also often misnamed tapestry.

A true tapestry is made on a loom, the design being an integral part of the cloth. What distinguishes tapestry from ordinary clothmaking is the way in which it is woven. *In clothmaking, warp and weft mingle in the fabric, but in tapestry the warp is completely hidden by the weft, which is well beaten down.*

Professional tapestry weavers use two kinds of loom: the *high-warp (haute-lisse)* which is a vertical upright loom, and the *low-warp (basse-lisse)* which is a horizontal loom worked by foot power. In traditional centres of tapestry weaving, where great ateliers still operate, weavers work on centuries-old looms. But tapestry can be woven on any loom on which plain cloth can be made. It is possible to weave small simple pieces on frames, and the standard 2-way and 4-shaft table looms are quite suitable for starting to explore the fascinations of tapestry.

Tapestry, by tradition, was woven sideways because horizontal lines are easier to weave than vertical ones. This meant that these horizontals appeared as verticals when the work was finished and hung on its weft. Nowadays, however, this is not always so. Tapestries are now often woven as they are meant to hang.

In true tapestry the wrong side of the work faces the weaver. This means that on a horizontal loom it is very difficult to see the weaving as it grows.

Making the Warp

When planning the dent, you must consider the scale of the design to be worked and the yarn to be used for warp and weft. A maximum of 8 dent is recommended for the beginner, using a medium flax or cotton yarn. Simple bold shapes can be worked on this dent using wefts of 3 ply, or 11 cut singles used double.

The bag woven on a 2-way loom (Fig. 9–3) was worked on warps of 6/2 cotton used double (5 dent, doubles) and wefts of a variety of double knit woollens, Aran yarn and carpet thrums.

As the warp is completely hidden, any colour can be used. The first requisite in a warp for tapestry is strength. When subjected to tension and heavy beating it must not snap, slip or fray. The material used for the warp has an effect on the finished cloth; linen warps make stiffer tapestries than cotton ones of the same thickness.

Weft Yarns

Weft yarns, forming the surface of the fabric, are all-important. By tradition, wool is the main weft yarn, but silk, cotton and synthetics can all be used. Experiment will show which yarns give the most surface texture. Beginners should use yarn of an even thickness throughout, progressing to fancy yarns, which can vary in thickness, when experience has been gained.

The weft yarns are used from bobbins (small shuttles), or from small bunches of yarn called *butterflies*. They are called butterflies because of the shape they make when the yarn is wound round the thumb and little finger. The end is looped round the bunch of yarn to secure it.

For simple tapestry projects like the ones described in this book, finish and join in yarns in the normal way. In complicated tapestry using many colours, the weft ends are not finished off but left dangling in lengths of 2 in. on the wrong side of the work.

Keeping an Even Edge

Check the sides of your tapestry frequently for gradual drawing in. If drawing in does occur it may be due to uneven tension of the warp, or too fine a weft yarn being used. Also check that the weft is not pulled too tightly across the shed before it is beaten down. To avoid this happening place the weft loosely in the shed, in an arc, before beating it down, and make sure that the weft fits neatly round the selvedges without forming loops, and without drawing in the warp strands. This fault is the most common one, particularly towards the end of the weaving, and the edges may begin to roll under as a consequence.

Bracing the tapestry with lengths of warp yarn stitched into the vertical edges of the work and attached to the side of the loom may help. Make these ties at intervals of 2 in. as the weaving grows.

Vertical Slit

(Fig. 9–4. Colour plate 10.)

This is a technique in which vertical slits are left between adjacent areas of weft colour. These slits may be small, formed by weaving a few picks only, in which case they are just left as small holes in the weave. Longer vertical slits are usually sewn up afterwards with a small stitch, invisible on the right side of the web. However in some places these slits are left to form an integral part of the design. The slit method is the best one to use where a clear definition of colour in vertical lines is needed in the design. The adjacent edges of the colour blocks are clean and clear-cut.

Work vertical slit technique like this (Fig. 9–5). The wefts move towards one another and touch, but do not interlock where they meet. When using more than two colours use each colour in turn from the left. Then deal with the short weft ends which protrude from the left of

Figs. 9–1a and b. Tapestry hangings (opposite and overleaf).

Fig. 9–2. *Tapestry mask with looped and plain pile* (previous page).

Fig. 9–3. *Striped tapestry bag with tassels. Made on a 2-way loom* (above).

Fig. 9–4. *Tapestry bag worked in vertical slit technique* (opposite).

each colour block by turning them back into the same shed. Beat and change the shed. Weave each colour back from right to left. Care must be taken not to pull in the individual small pieces of weaving too much or the vertical line between the colour changes will not be straight.

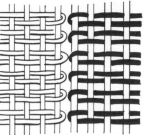

Fig. 9–5. *Tapestry, vertical slit.*

Diagonal Slit

(Figs. 9–6 and 9–7. Colour plate 1.)

With this method the technique is almost the same as for vertical slit. The only difference is that the weft yarns move further one way as the pattern is woven. This means that no further treatment of the slits is necessary; the colours join in a diagonal line as the slits are always very small.

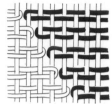

Fig. 9–6. Tapestry, diagonal slit.

Diagonals can be worked on pairs or groups of weft picks. This alters the angle of the diagonal line between the colours. The slits become a little longer as the number of picks worked before turning increases. Several picks of one side can be woven before the second colour is woven to the same level. This method is quicker than working a

Fig. 9–7. Example of diagonal slit technique (below).

pick at a time. Be careful to work out the correct order of shapes if you are weaving a design in which shapes slope inwards and outwards. Always weave the inward slopes first. If you don't do this, you may finish with small shapes of warp strings left unwoven, and no means of weaving them except darning them in with a needle.

Interlocked Weft

(Fig. 9–8.)

This is a technique of colour change which also gives clear outlines. The difference between this technique and the slit weaving technique is that, where the colours touch one another, the wefts lock. Using two colours from opposite selvedges, lock the wefts where they meet, and return the colours to the selvedges in the opposite shed.

Fig. 9–8. Interlocked weft.

If several colours are planned, or if a checkerboard design made of two weft colours is planned, work as follows. Open the shed and lay into it all the weft threads from left to right. The pick will now consist of short lengths of weft in the various colours lying in the shed, with the shuttles or butterflies of yarn on the right, and the short ends of weft protruding from the web on the left. Deal with the short weft ends first by finishing them off in the same shed position. Then change the shed, weave the first right-hand section of weft colour to its boundary, and lock this colour round the second weft colour. Lay the first colour shuttle on top of the work and weave with the next colour across the second area. Between colours two and three lock the wefts again and continue in this way until the left-hand selvedge is reached. The pick will now consist of short passages of various weft colours, all locked round each other at their right edges, but with the shuttles or butterflies of yarn coming from their left edges.

Change the shed, after beating, and weave back across each colour, using the shuttles in turn, but without interlocking, until the right-hand selvedge is reached.

Beat and change the shed and weave again to the left, this time locking all the wefts in turn.

Care must be taken to ensure that the wefts lock in exactly the same place each time, between the 2 warp ends. If one weft colour is pulled more than the other, this interlocking line will not be central between the 2 warp ends.

Vertical Dovetail
(Fig. 9–9.)
With this method, the weft yarns wrap round a common warp end at the turning points, instead of wrapping round one another in the space between 2 warp ends.

Take the two colours of wefts from opposite selvedges and turn them round the same warp end. Beat, change the shed and return the wefts to the selvedge. This is single dovetailing, but it is quite possible to turn 2 or 3 picks of weft round the common warp end.

When dovetail joins are used, the boundary edge is saw-toothed and less clear-cut than with slit or weft lock technique.

Due to the constant wrapping of 2 weft yarns round the same warp thread at the same place, a ridge forms where the colours meet.

Fig. 9–9. Vertical dovetail.

Skip Plain Weave
(Figs. 9–10 and 9–11. Colour plate 12.)
If a reversible fabric is not needed, there is a quick and easy way to weave squares or straight sided figures.

Weave a section of cloth in one colour only. Decide on the number and width of the squares. Raise the shafts, and using one colour on the shuttle take it into the shed where it is needed and under the web, forming a float where it

Fig. 9–10. Tapestry using skip plain weave and knotting.

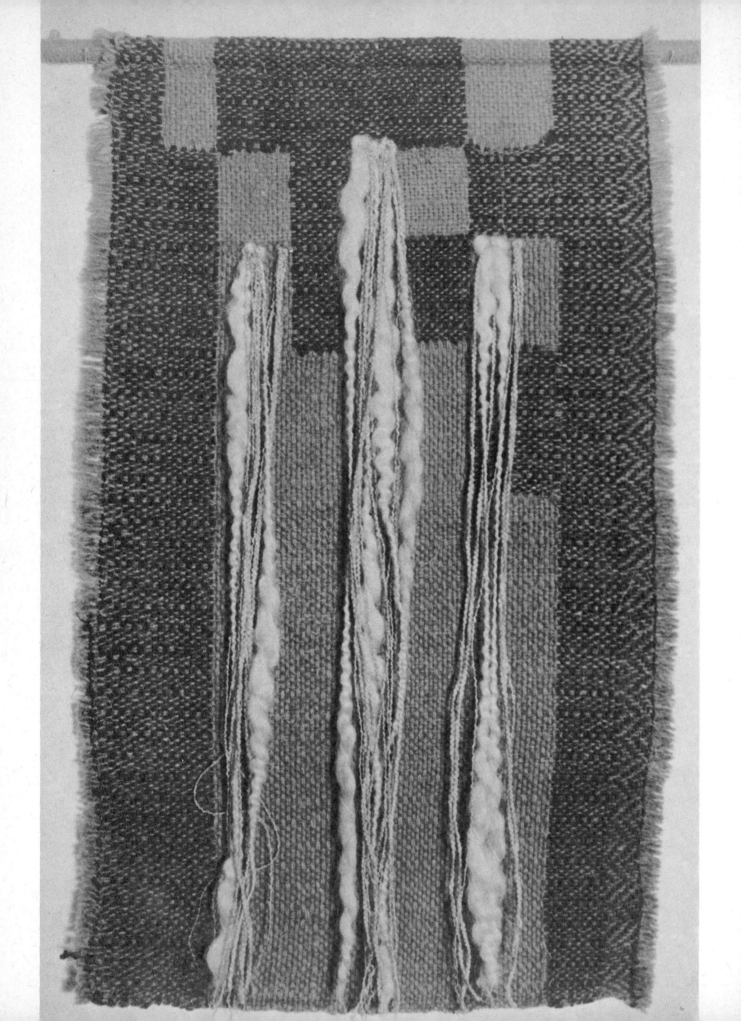

will not show. Keeping the same shafts raised, introduce the second colour, weaving it into the shed where the first weft is under the web. Conversely, this second colour should float underneath when the first colour occupies that section of the shed. The pick of weaving should consist of equal sections of shed in each colour, with floats under the web. Beat, change the shed and repeat.

Broad stripes can be woven like this, and squares can be woven by reversing the colour order. This method can be used on normal cloth sett as well.

Fig. 9–11. Wall hanging using skip plain weave. This is really a tapestry technique, normally used with close beating (opposite).

Weaving a Tapestry Sampler

Set up a narrow warp using double ends of 2/4 or 2/6 mercerized cotton. Work a sampler, including the following techniques:
(1) Practise beating to ensure complete warp coverage and an even selvedge.
(2) Use two colours, pick and pick, which will produce vertical stripes (Fig. 1–4 and Colour plate 9).
(3) Reverse the colour order.

Fig. 9–12. Strip weaving using skip plain weave on a tie-dyed warp with macramé (below).

(4) Weave in *meet-and-separate* technique. Use slit weave, i.e. don't lock the wefts. Take colour A half-way across the warp. Bring colour B, in the same shed, from the opposite selvedge to meet colour A. Beat, and change the shed. Return each colour to its original selvedge in this shed. On successive picks move the point at which the two weft colours meet and separate.

Crossing the colours at the meeting point, so that the colour changes from one side of the cloth to the other, produces an attractive variation on this technique.

(5) Skein some wool the same width as the warp, and tie-dye it (see Chapter 12). When woven, it will form interesting blocks of colour in the weave.

(6) Use knotting to raise a pile on the weave.

(7) Weave an angular shape, triangle or diamond, using diagonal slit technique.

(8) Weave a small square or rectangle using vertical slit technique. Sew the slits up afterwards. When weaving, take care to keep the edges straight.

(9) Make a low semi-circular shape by building up the shape in the middle, i.e. decreasing the width of the semi-circle gradually. Don't make the base of the shape too wide. Instead of filling in each side with a background yarn, weave the complete pick from selvedge to selvedge, letting the weft pack down loosely on top of the semi-circle. Wedge shapes can be built up at the sides, and the whole fabric will be made up of curving weft rows instead of normal horizontal picks. Beat with the fingers or the tip of the shuttle.

Fig. 9–13. Meet-and-separate technique.

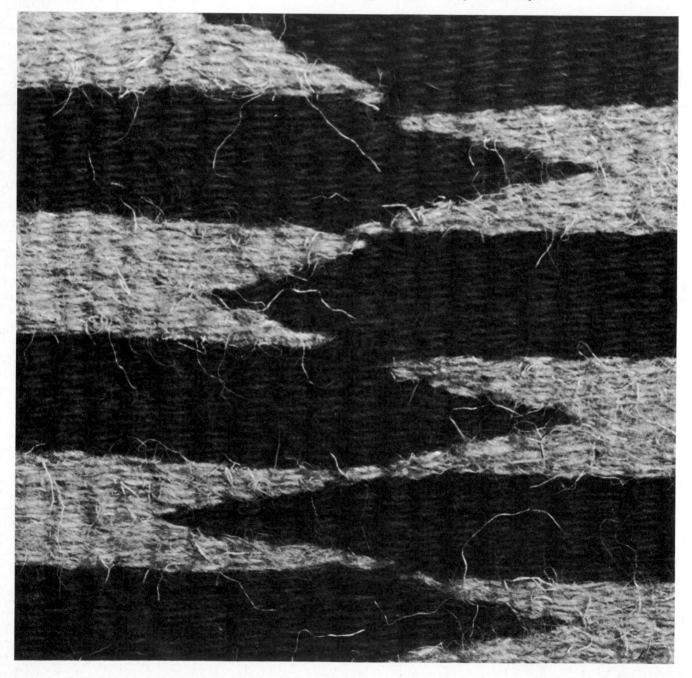

10. Denting

THE DENTS IN THE REED are the *spaces between the metal strips*, and *denting is the way in which the warp threads are placed in these spaces*. Reeds are available from fine to coarse. The standard reed supplied with the Dryad Cottage loom is 14 dent, and the one supplied with the standard Harris table loom is 8 dent. Both firms can supply a wide range of reeds on request (see *Suppliers*).

The purpose for which the cloth is designed and the thickness of warp and weft yarns to be used must be considered when planning the dent of a warp. The pattern to be used also has an effect. In plain weave there are more yarn intersections to an inch, which means that a slightly coarser sett will be required than with twill. A coarse reed is more useful than a fine one, because paired ends on a coarse reed are the usual practice in handweaving, rather than single *sleying* with a finer reed.

Denting with an 8 dent reed

8 dent	single across the reed i.e. 1 per dent	8 ends per inch
12 dent	2, 1, 2, 1, etc. in alternate dents	12 ends per inch
16 dent	double across the reed i.e. 2 per dent	16 ends per inch
20 dent	2, 3, 2, 3, etc. in alternate dents	20 ends per inch
24 dent	treble across the reed i.e. 3 per dent	24 ends per inch
28 dent	3, 4, 3, 4, etc. in alternate dents	28 ends per inch

Denting with a 14 dent reed

14 dent	single across the reed i.e. 1 per dent	14 ends per inch
21 dent	2, 1, 2, 1, etc. in alternate dents	21 ends per inch
28 dent	double across the reed i.e. 2 per dent	28 ends per inch
35 dent	2, 3, 2, 3, etc. in alternate dents	35 ends per inch
42 dent	treble across the reed i.e. 3 per dent	42 ends per inch

Variety in the density of denting can make interesting cloth. *Cramming* (Fig. 10–2) means having more than the normal number of warp ends for the weight of yarn in each dent, and *spacing* (Figs. 8–27, 10–3, 10–4 and 10–5) occurs when small areas of the reed are left empty. Spacing and cramming used in the same warp will vary the texture and colour of the cloth, and heavy and light beating of the weft can match warp density. Warp ends which are to be taken through the same dent in the reed should be entered singly in the heddles and then grouped together at the reed. With spacing, keep a firm band of normal denting at each selvedge, and limit the width and number of the spaces left empty in the reed.

The denting of every piece should be noted for reference. Charts for denting are usually worked from right to left and added to the pattern draft. One way of showing irregular distribution of ends in the reed is to bracket the number of warp ends to be entered in each dent of the reed.

Most weavers will find an 8 dent reed the most useful to begin with, but may wish to buy an extra reed for finer work as they progress. Reeds are interchangeable on looms, and it is certainly useful to have more than one.

Warp Setts

The warp *sett (the number of warp ends to the inch)* depends on the cloth chosen as well as on the size of warp and weft yarns. Correct setting is an art. If in doubt, wind the warp yarn round a 1 in. width on a ruler so that the threads touch but don't overlap. Count the number of threads in an inch and divide by 2. This will give you the correct *dent*. The following table will help.

Cotton		Wool		
4/2 }		11 cut 14—20 }		
	14—21	16 cut 20—22	} Galashiels	
6/2 }				
18/3	26—28	25 cut 26—28 }		

N.B. The lower number in each case is for a tabby cloth.

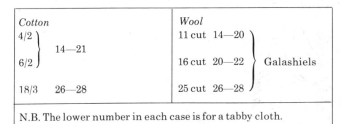
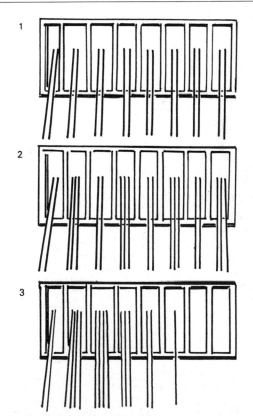

Fig. 10–1. Three ways of using an 8 dent reed.
(1) The threads are double across the reed (16 dent).
(2) The threads have been placed in the dents of the reed in twos and threes alternately (20 dent).
(3) Reading from the left, the threads have been placed as follows: 2, 3, 4, 3, 2, 1, 0, 0.

Fig. 10–2. Fancy yarns, warp crammed in the reed (below). Fig. 10–3. Tie-dyed warp with lace ovals (opposite).

Fig. 10–4. Centre of an altar frontal in white, pale greys and
brilliant lime yellow, to be mounted on dark cloth. The centre of the
cross is accentuated by squares cut from large silver sequins
(opposite).

Fig. 10–5. Semi-transparent curtaining on a spaced warp.
Handspun and natural dyed wool in the weft. Monksbelt (below).

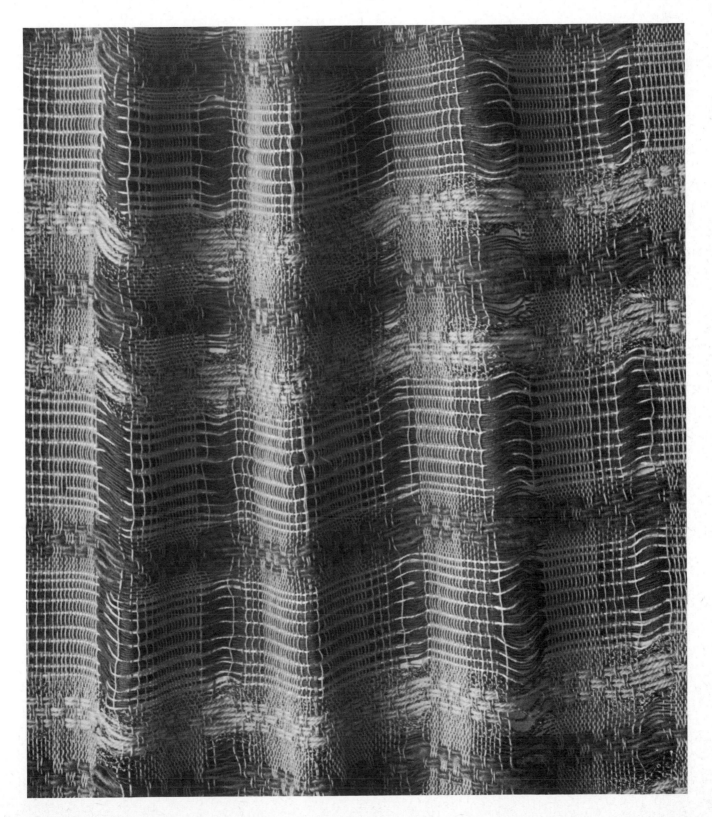

11. How to Make Some of the Articles in This Book

Hanging with Strip Weaving and Macramé

(Fig. 11–1.)
Finished width: 18 in.
Finished length: 48 in.
Draft: twill.
Dent: 14, *using double threads.*
Yarn: warp 6/2 mercerized cotton, flame.
   weft Crysette, and Strutt's glacé cotton, black.

THE TOP OF THE WARP is tie-dyed in a checkerboard pattern, and the fringe is also tie-dyed to give flecks of flame through the black. Cut 12 strips of metallic plastic or thin leather (18 in. × 2 in.) and thin card (18 in. × 1 in.). Using an instant impact adhesive, make up the strips and cover two mild steel rods with leather or plastic cut to size. Place the joins where they will not be visible. Weave with the Strutt's glacé cotton and the metallic strips. Pass the strips on top of the warp ends as in Fig. 11–1 to make a checkerboard pattern. Weave 1 pick of soumak between each strip and darken some of the checks with macramé (flat knots and bannisters) worked over the warp ends. Brighten others by stitching metal threads across the strips in the same direction as the warp. Insert the rods at top and bottom for extra weight. Fringe with macramé, and leather and ceramic beads.

Tapestry Hanging Using Vertical Slit Technique and Macramé

(Fig. 9–1b. Colour plate 7.)
Finished width: 22 in.
Finished length: 35 in.
Draft: twill.
Dent: 5.
Yarn: warp flax warp twine.
   weft 2 ply carpet wool in natural, double knitting wool, gimps, dyed sisal, unspun nylon sliver, velvet chenille, linen, Courtelle slubs.

This kind of work, using deep-textured fringes, needs the yarn to be dyed before weaving is started.
 Using as many different types and thicknesses of yarn as you can, tie and knot them in a variety of ways in whatever colour scheme you have in mind. In this example the colours include navy blue, brown, rust, deep yellow, olive and rose. The lighter tones are pale shades of pink, stone, natural and many different types of white yarn. Some yarns are all one colour and others are striped and speckled by tie-dyeing.
 The rectangular motifs are worked in vertical slit technique; the background cloth is made more interesting by the use of natural textured yarns and macramé worked in bannisters over some of the warp ends. The weaving is done first, and the macramé is done afterwards on the empty warp threads. Start by knotting the threads for macramé round a group of warp ends, at the top, close to the edge of the weaving. Then work bannisters along the length of warp. The fringe is bound in places with shiny embroidery silk in vermilion, yellow, olive, dull pink and navy.

Hanging in Plain Weave and Gauze or Leno

(Fig. 11–2.)
Finished width: 14 in.
Finished length: 33 in.
Draft: twill on 4 shafts.
Dent: 28.
Yarn: warp and weft 12/2 cotton.
N.B. Allow enough warp length for the macramé fringe – about four times the length of the final fringe.

The warp consists of irregular stripes of uneven thickness in twelve colours: purple, dark blue, several shades of blue and mauve, green and pink. The width of the stripes varies from 4 to 16 ends, and the subtle shift of colour is carried through into the fringe by the macramé. All gauze weave is worked by twisting 4 over 4.
 The top section (5 in.) and the bottom section (8 in.) are worked in dark purple plain weave alternating with bands of gauze. The middle section (8 in.) has some rectangular shapes in gauze, the rest being in plain weave using jade green cotton. In two places the warp strands are left unwoven.
 The macramé fringe should be worked with 8 warp ends grouped together to serve as a thicker yarn. The knots used are straight and diagonal cording, single and interlacing flat knots and bannisters. Finish the ends in plaits.

Striped Tapestry Bag with Tassels

(Fig. 9–3.)
Finished width: 13 in.
Finished length: 22 in. (folded in half).
Draft: plain weave on a 2-way loom.
Dent: 5, *using double threads.*
Yarn: warp 6/2 cotton.
   weft Aran wool and oddments of double knitting wool.

Woven with the stripes running across, the bag is made up by folding the length sideways, so that the stripes run down the bag from top to bottom. Make the fringe at the top by turning down the woven edge, stitching on a sewing machine and fraying the weft ends out. Finish with a plait strengthened with firm ribbon or binding, and tassels.

Fig. 11–1. Metallic strip weave (opposite).

Fig. 11–2. Multi-coloured hanging in plain weave, gauze weave and macramé (overleaf).

Twill Bags in Tapestry

(Figs. 11–3, 11–4 and 11–5.)

Finished size: whatever the weaver chooses.

Dent: 5.

Yarn: warp flax warp twine.

      weft 2 ply carpet wool.

These bags are woven in 2/2 twill using a sequence of 12 picks, with two colours.

Starting with colour A, weave as follows (reading downwards):

43	colour A	43	colour A	43	colour A
32	colour B	32	colour B	32	colour B
21	colour B	21	colour A	21	colour B
14	colour A	14	colour A	14	colour B

The fringed bag in navy and white has the bands running across it. The sequence of colour is reversed after every 12 picks.

The other bag, in tan and white, uses the 12 pick colour sequence with stripes of the same two colours. This bag is made up by folding the cloth at the side, and stitching it together.

Fig. 11–3. Detail of Fig. 11–4 (overleaf).

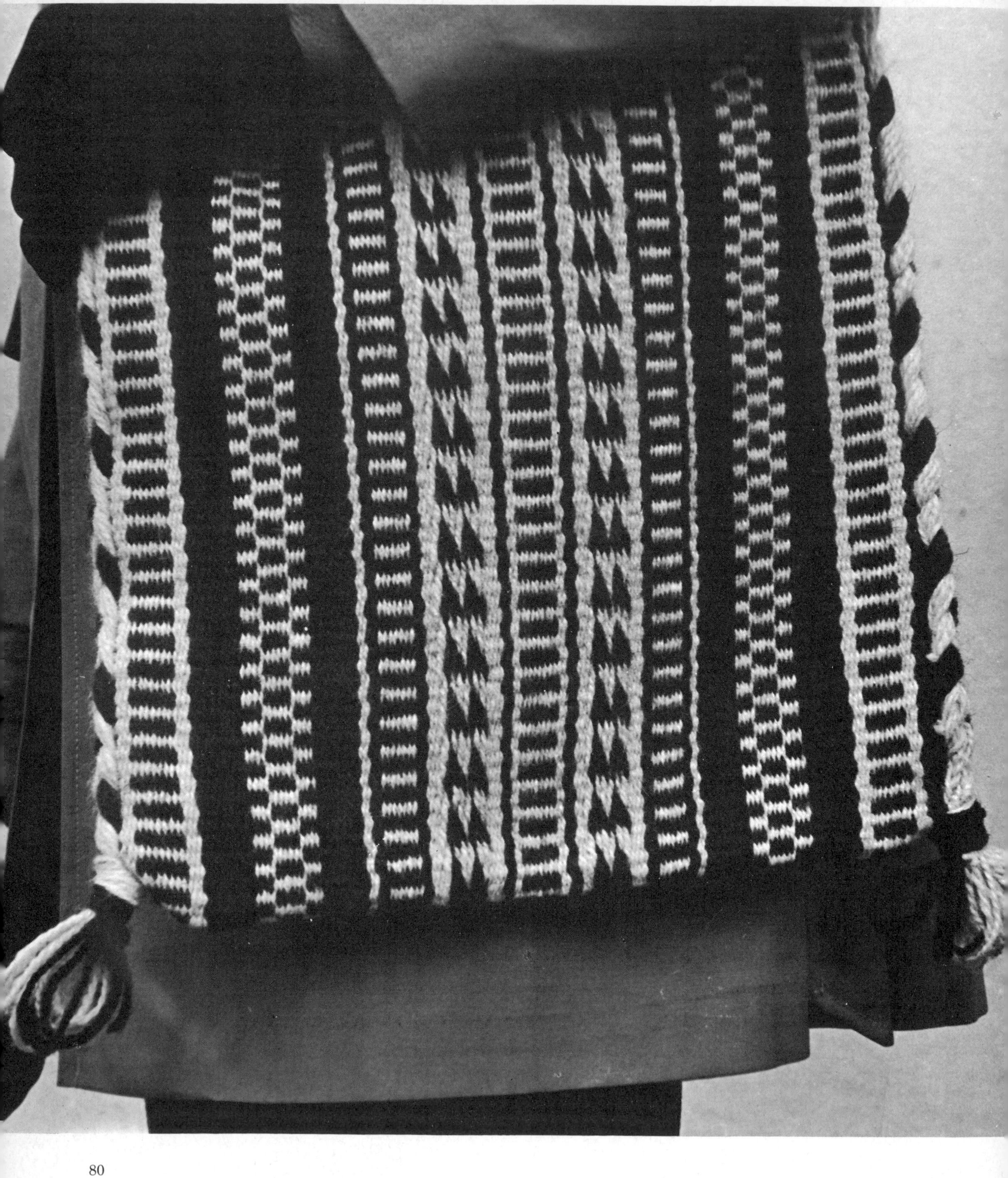

Hanging Using Plain Weave, Spanish Lace and Knotting

(Fig. 11–6. Colour plate 13.)
Finished width: 28 in.
Finished length: 48 in.
Draft: twill.
Dent: 14, in 5 even sections, spaced with 6 empty dents in between the warp.
Yarn: warp 6/2 mercerized cotton in two shades of yellow.
weft 6/2 mercerized cotton, brighter yellow worsted slub, grey effect woollen gimp/black cotton, several tones of fine linen from tan to cream, worsted gimp.

Worked from the bottom, the design is stepped up from the middle. The Spanish lace, worked double, follows the same line. Spanish lace alternates with ovals drawn up with the woollen gimp/black cotton. The tufting from the Ghiordes knots contains a variety of yarns; all tufts should be trimmed level.

Fig. 11–6. Hanging in plain weave, Spanish lace and knotting (opposite).

Hanging Using Batik Patterned Stripes

(Fig. 11–7. Colour plate 14.)
Finished width: 26 in.
Finished length: 39 in.
Draft: twill.
Dent: 14, spaced.
Yarn: warp and weft 4/2 cotton, brown and navy.

Cut a piece of washed cotton cloth 54 in. long. Tape it to a table and draw a large circle on it (use a pencil tied to a piece of string). Pin the cloth on an old picture frame to produce a taut surface on which to work. Heat some candles in a double saucepan until the wax is hot but not boiling. *Never heat wax in a single saucepan.* Paint the hot wax on the cloth in a circular design. (To avoid unwanted spots on the cloth carry the brush over a lid or rng held in your other hand). Dye in yellow, wax again and dye in rust. Use cold water Dylon dyes or the Procion M range. Remove the wax by ironing through several layers of shelf paper above and underneath the cloth (for Dylon), or by boiling it off (for Procion M). Make up the strips using thin card to stiffen them, keeping the joins on the wrong side. Weave. Use yellow embroidery silk to stitch across some of the strips, parallel to the warp. Add a rod at the top for hanging, and finish the fringe by wrapping the warp in places with white, yellow and rust embroidery silk.

Lectern Cloth

(Colour plate 11.)
Finished width: 23 in.
Finished length: 30 in.
Draft: twill.
Dent: this varies between 28 and 14, according to the count of the yarn used.

Yarn: warp 6/2 and 12/2 cotton in black, wine, brown, scarlet and vermilion, used 1/1 throughout.
weft wool in royal blue, black, scarlet, vermilion and orange; pink gimp, copper lurex, gold snarl, and fine speckled lurex and wool in pink and dark blue.

The dent of the cloth varies with the count of the yarn. Two alternating colours are used in turn in the warp, causing the colour to change gradually across the warp from dark to bright and back to dark. Starting at the edge with black and dark wine, end and end, the black is replaced by brown, then brown by scarlet, then scarlet by vermilion; finally, the wine is replaced by scarlet again, this section being the brightest in the warp. The colour then starts all over again. Weave in plain weave.

The ribbed effect in the cloth, caused by using a thick weft, is emphasized when the dent is finest. The inlay sections are executed in lurex or fine speckled wool and lurex. As these yarns are flimsy, include a fine cotton or wool yarn in each pick. The inlay is worked with a weft lock technique but without hard beating. Double weft threads are used throughout, and to make up the same thickness as the shuttle the inlay is worked with 3 strands.

Interline the work when it is finished, and then line with a non-slip material, such as felt.

Fig. 11–7. Batik printed strip weave on a spaced warp (overleaf).

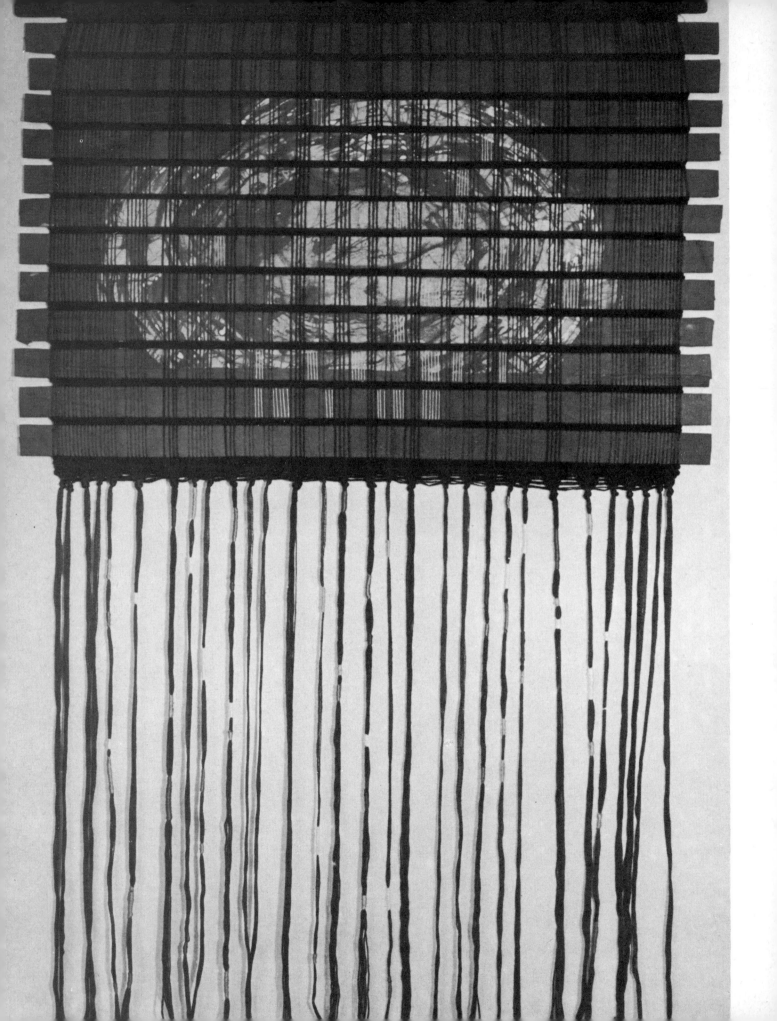

12. Colour and Decoration in Weaving

Colour

CHOICE OF COLOUR is always a personal matter. Some weavers use colour instinctively while others find selection difficult. Nature can provide unlimited inspiration for colour, proportion in design and surface texture. Look at things about you. Study the work of painters and craftsmen and spend some time experimenting with paint or dyes on paper. Above all experiment on your loom. The beginner may find it helpful to keep to groups of colours, e.g. warm tones ranging through pinks and browns to orange, or cool tones, restricting your work perhaps to the many shades of grey, finishing with black. Remember that very pale colours used on a dark warp appear almost white and lose their true delicacy, while dark tones seem darker than they are on a light warp. Experience is the best teacher. In addition, try to resist including too many techniques in one piece of work; one idea for one piece of work is a good rule to follow. Be simple – it is the secret of good design.

Painting, Printing and Tie-Dyeing

There are close links between weaving and textile printing. Usually the patterning is done on the warp either before or after it is stretched on the loom. *Painting a warp* can be done with waterproof drawing inks or with thin dye colour. Fabric dyes such as Dylon or Procion are recommended for *tie-dyeing*, and Polyprint colours, easily fixed by ironing, for *block or screen printing* (Colour plate 2).

For *screen printing,* stretch the warp out on a table and tape it down firmly. Then print the design. This will dirty the table so newspaper should be spread on the table before you start to print. Take great care when you print the design and transfer the warp to the loom, otherwise the design may slip. It is easier, in fact, to print a small length of warp at a time, *after* the warp is stretched on the loom. Use the warp at the front between the shafts and reed. First, take the beater frame off the reed or tie the reed to the front beam. Roll the warp on so that the design will print where you would expect to start weaving. Directly underneath the taut warp build up a platform of books or cardboard boxes and place a sheet of card on top, cut to the correct size. Print, using blocks or screens, and allow to dry. Before rolling on the next area for printing, secure the design by inserting a few temporary weft picks at intervals. Circular shapes, which are difficult to weave, can be most effective in printed warps, but colours must be chosen carefully to fit the warp yarn and also the proposed weft.

Tie-dyeing a warp is easy and can make simple weaving look very complex. Before making the warp decide what you want to do. If, as in Fig. 12–1, large ovals are planned in the warp, make the warp in 3 separate sections, and tie off each of the 3 warps on the warping posts. Then tie up the middle section, using strong plastic and linen yarn.

Fig. 12 1. Tie dyed warp, gauze weave and inlay.

In Fig. 12–2, the warp has been made in many small, separate sections and tied up to form a checkerboard of squares. (This technique could be very interesting used with a decorative square pattern like monksbelt, or with inlay.) Tie the warp either on the warping posts, or by laying it flat on a table. Dye according to the instructions provided with your dyes. In Fig. 12–3, the warp of brilliant scarlet needed two Dylon dyes (black over red) to achieve

the correct depth of colour.

To tie-dye the weft, skein the yarn to the same width as the warp, tie and dye.

Fig. 12–2. Warp tied ready for dyeing (below).

Fig. 12–3. A tie-dyed warp. Untie a few at a time and roll on (opposite).

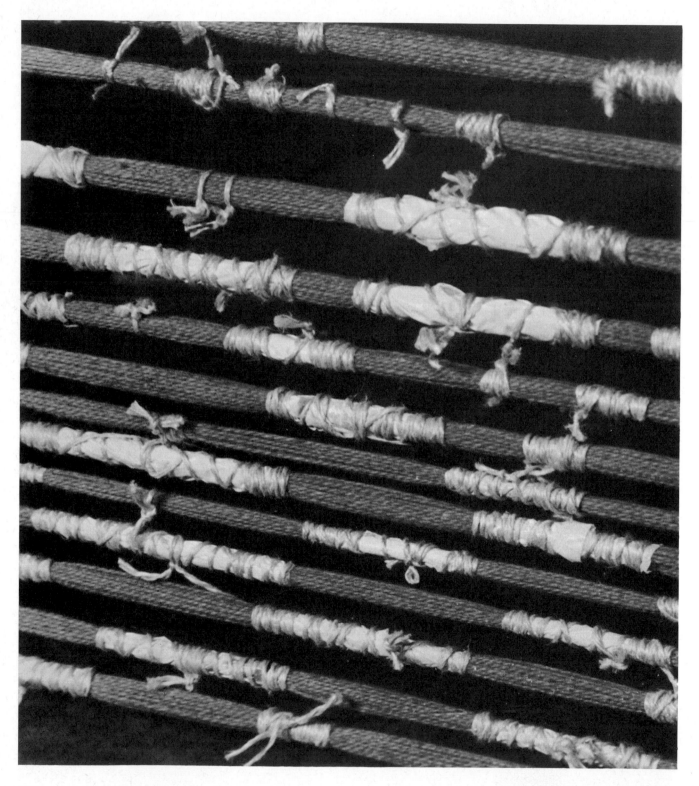

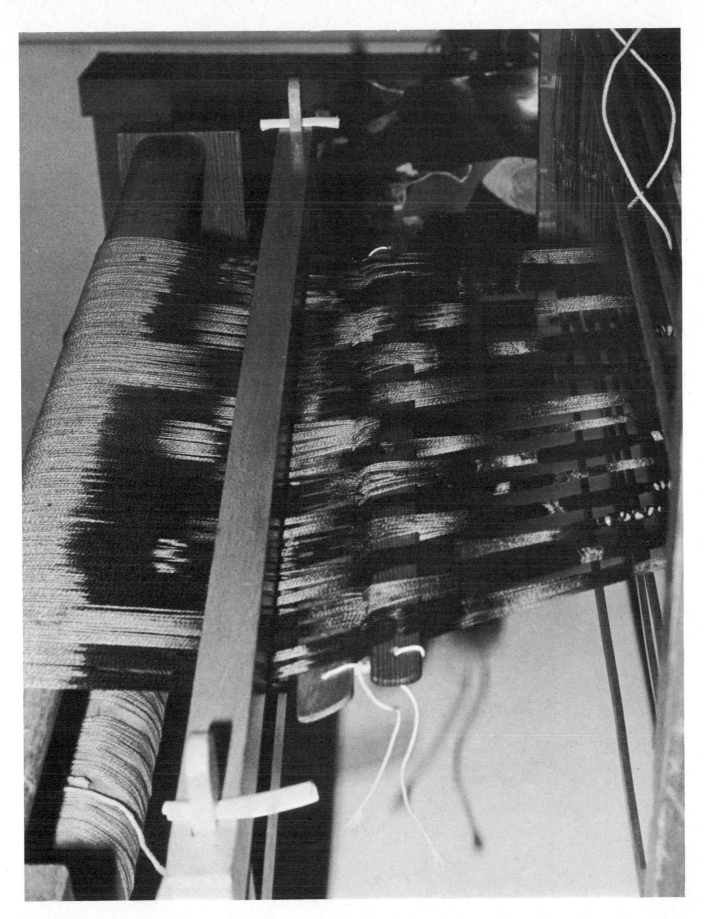

Fig. 12–4. Centre of a woven panel. The warp is printed and sections of it left unwoven. Buttonhole stitch (opposite).

Fig. 12–5. Tie-dyed warp with inlay (below).

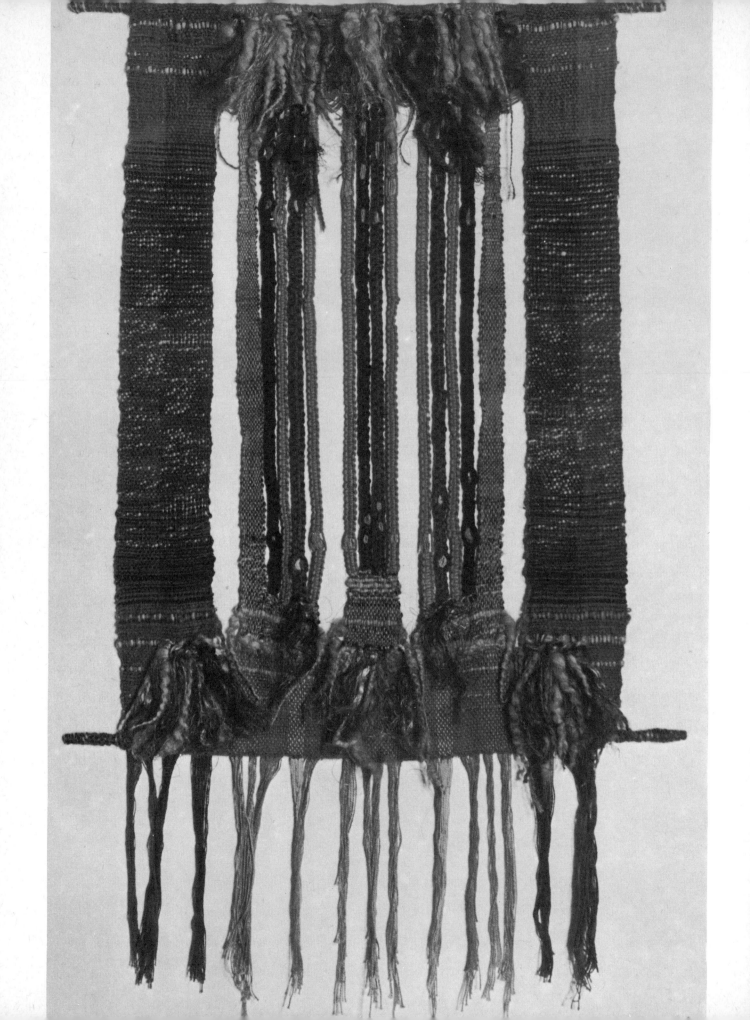

Using Macramé with Weaving

(Colour plates 15 and 16.)

Macramé is a natural craft to combine with weaving. There are many books which show the basic macramé knots (see *Recommended Books*). Flat knots or bannisters can be made on groups of warp ends or as a fringe. Beads used in the knotting should be strung on an additional thread knotted round the group of warp ends being used. Figs. 12–6—12–10 show a variety of uses of macramé with weaving.

Fig. 12–6. Hanging woven with slits, macramé worked over the warp strands. Woven on a 2-way loom (opposite).

Fig. 12–7. Circular weaving on a card loom with macramé edge (below).

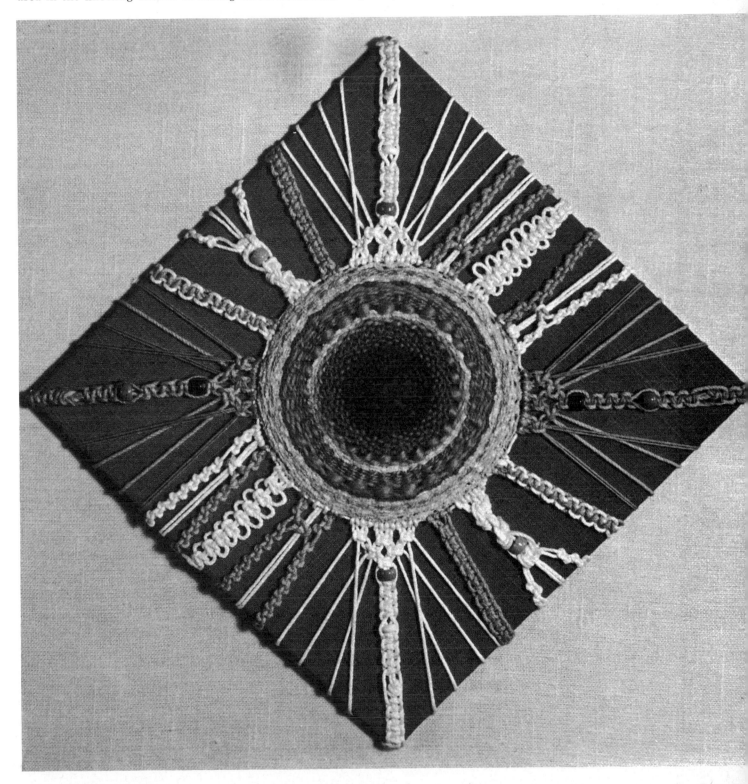

Fig. 12–9. *Detail of macramé fringe* (opposite).

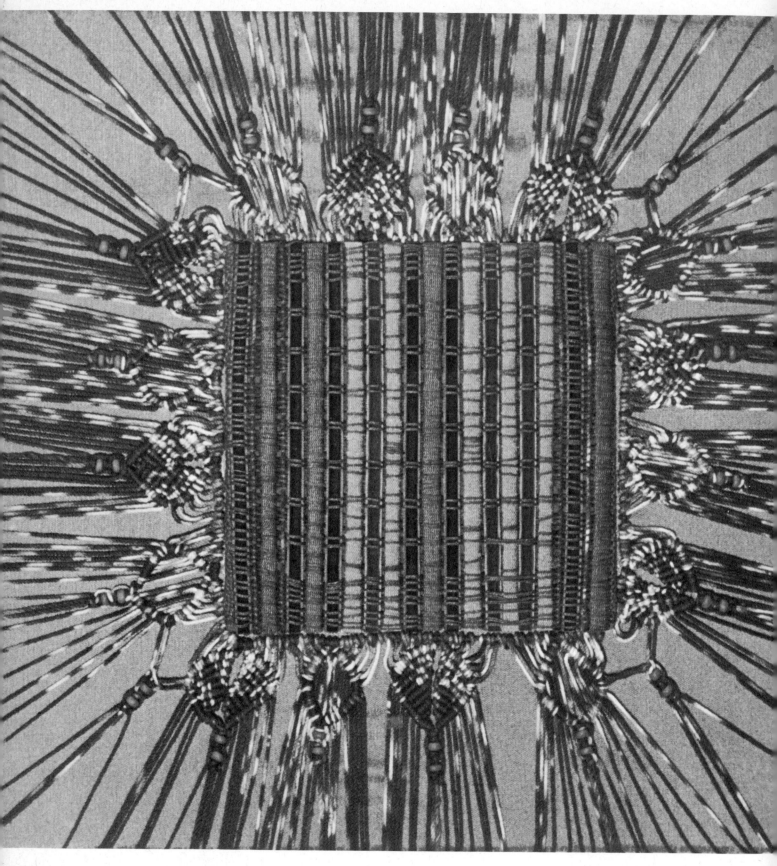

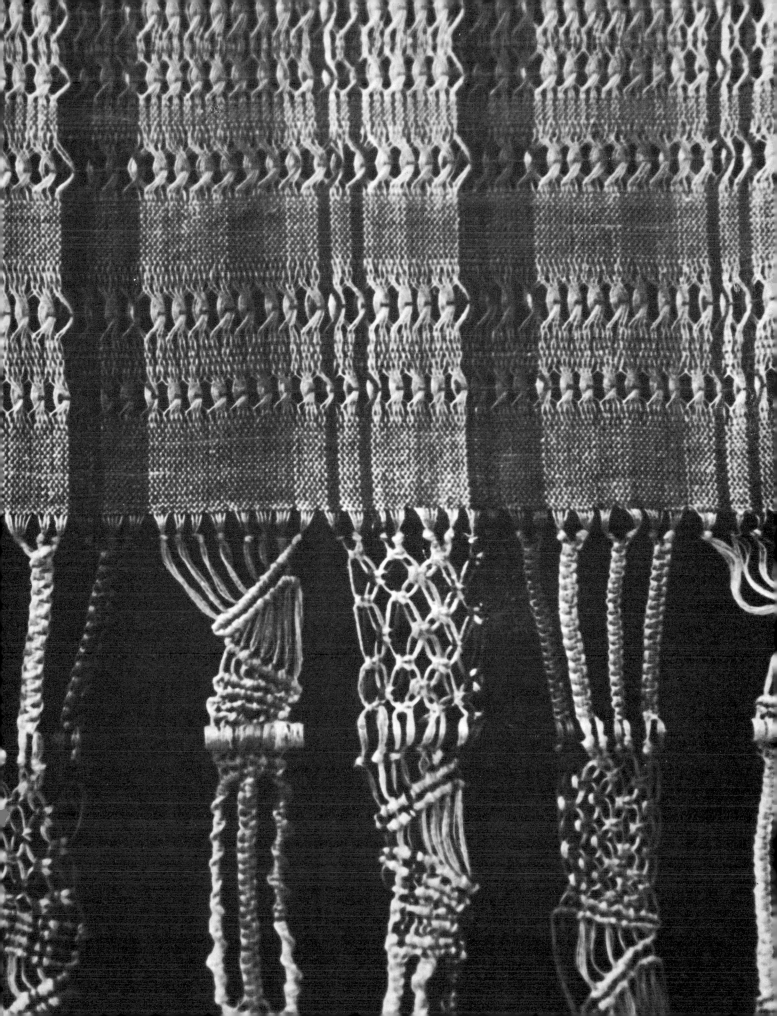

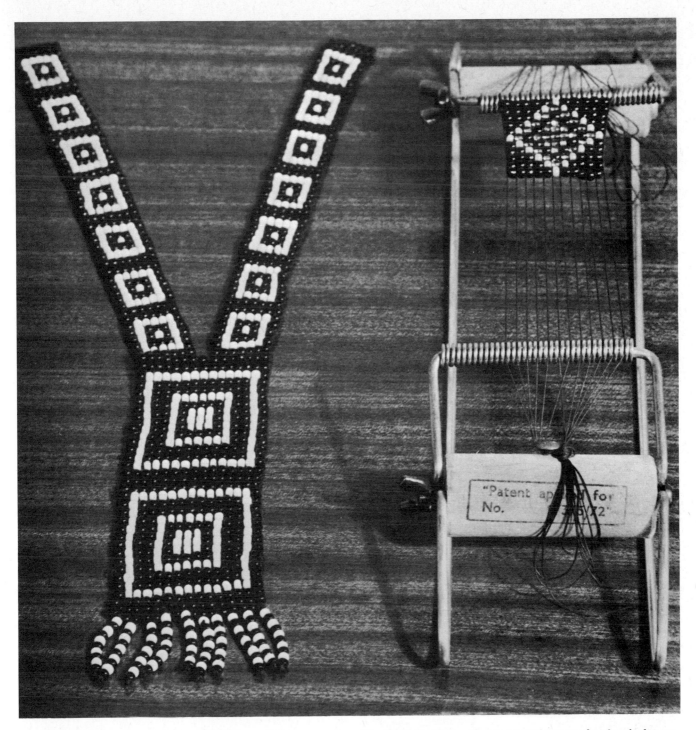

Fig. 12–10. Spaced warp, macramé and beads (opposite).

Fig. 12–11. Bead loom, showing warp in every other dent for larger beads (above).

Bead Weaving

(Fig. 12–11.)

Designs for bead weaving should be worked out on squared paper; the lines between the squares represent the warp. The warp ends must be spaced to fit the width of the bead, but no proper sheds are formed to weave. This makes it easy to improvise simple bead looms. Use strong cotton passed through beeswax to make it even stronger. Its thickness will depend on the hole in the bead and the needle used. Cut the warp 20 in. longer than the intended

length of the piece of weaving, and put it on the loom. To weave, tie the weft thread to the left warp end and thread with the correct sequence of beads for the first pick. Bring the thread to the right, *underneath the warp*, pushing the beads into their correct positions between the warp threads. Hold the beads there with the index finger of the left hand while threading the cotton from right to left, over each warp thread and through each eye of the beads. This completes a pick. When you have finished, thread the weft ends back through the beads so that they are secure.

13. Further Ideas

WHEN YOU HAVE COMPLETED your first piece of cloth you may not yet feel very expert, but *you will know how to weave*. The processes of warping, setting up the loom and actually weaving have been done once. Practice now will make them easier and quicker to do.

(1) Now try weaving with wool (see Appendix A), taking extra care in handling the warp at all stages. Use strong yarn to start with: because of the oil in which it is soaked, tweed singles yarn is as easy to use as a plied wool; 11 cut, 3 or 4 ply used 13, 14 or 16 dent would also be a good choice. Instead of using a single colour, as in your first warp, try using two.

(2) You could consider making a bag in log cabin weave. Combine two contrasting yarns, warping the two threads together (see Appendix A). Thread in log cabin pattern, and try alternating the two contrasting colours in your weaving.

(3) Divide your warp into 3 parts using three similar colours for each third, e.g. natural, yellow and orange; three shades of pink; turquoise, jade and blue, or any other combination that appeals to you. Weave in the same shades, using each colour for one third of the weft. The square pattern produced could be outlined by including 2 warp threads and 2 weft picks in a dark contrast between each colour.

This would make an attractive cushion cover.

Fig. 13–1. Cushion cover with surface texture using fancy weft yarns (opposite).

(4) Another cushion cover could be made on the same warp, but using a weft of thick and thin fancy yarn throughout over the warp colours. The cushion in Fig. 13–1 was woven in a thick slub and thin gimp in natural and brilliant pink, over a warp made from four tones of neutral beiges and greys. When making this warp, join as described in Appendix A.

(5) With a 4-shaft loom the choice for second pieces of work is wider. Not only can you use any of the patterns given, but you have an opportunity to extend your knowledge by varying the density of the dent (see Chapter 10).

Appendix A
Weaving with Wool

Friction. Warping with wool can cause friction between the warp ends as they pass through the cross, resulting in small balls of wool appearing between the cross sticks. These must be removed as they will prevent the warp running through the cross. Separate the threads at the cross by pulling them gently sideways away from one another, and then pick off any small balls of wool (Fig. A–1).

Fig. A–1. Separating woollen warp ends by pulling the threads away from one another (below).

Warping with Two Crosses. Wool warps can be made with a single cross and beamed on to the back of the loom, the threads in the warp being passed through the cross. There is also an alternative method using two crosses, and beaming through the raddle; this is for a 4-shaft loom.

By moving the pegs, set up the warping frame for the right length. If you are using warping posts you will need two crosses, so use two double posts to make a cross at both ends. As the warp here is to be threaded in pairs through an 8 dent reed (16 dent), the threads must be separated into groups of ends holding 8 threads (Fig. A–2) – enough for one space in the raddle.

Fig. A–2. Marking the warp threads in groups of 8.

When the correct number of threads has been warped, secure both crosses (Fig. A–3). As the end cross (A) is where the warp will be tied to the loom, put a stick (the correct length for the loom) through the end loop. To this stick tie a string which passes through the other loop. The first cross (B) must also be secured, because the sequence of threads there will be needed for threading the heddles. Either encircle the cross with one string through both loops, or tie 4 separate strings round each layer of the cross threads.

Chain the warp from this first cross (Fig. A–4). Raddle by placing the groups of 8 threads in each space (Fig. A–5). When the threads are safely in the raddle with the top secured, pull off the marker cord (Fig. A–6). With the warp on the raddle, tie the stick to the back of the loom at each side only. Arrange the warp threads along the back stick as they are in the raddle, and complete the ties (Fig. A–7). Note that the shafts have been removed to create space through which to pass the warp; the reed in its batten has

been pushed forward. Fig. A–8 shows the warp tied to the back of the loom with beaming just started.

Hold the warp taut and smooth out any tangles. Then comb the raddle forward through the warp. Push the raddle to the back of the loom and wind on the smoothed warp. Tighten the yarn round the back beam by pulling steadily on the warp. Repeat until the warp is rolled on, leaving about 20 in. of warp, including a cross, at the front of the loom. Replace the ties of this cross with sticks (Fig. A–9) and remove the raddle. Replace the shafts and having cut the threads of warp into single ends, thread the heddles and reed and complete the tie-up.

Fig. A–3. The completed warp, showing the marking of threads in eights for counting. One cross has been tied up with four separate pieces of cord to secure it. At the second cross a stick has been placed in one loop, and a cord tied to it through the other loop. This stick will be tied to the back of the loom.

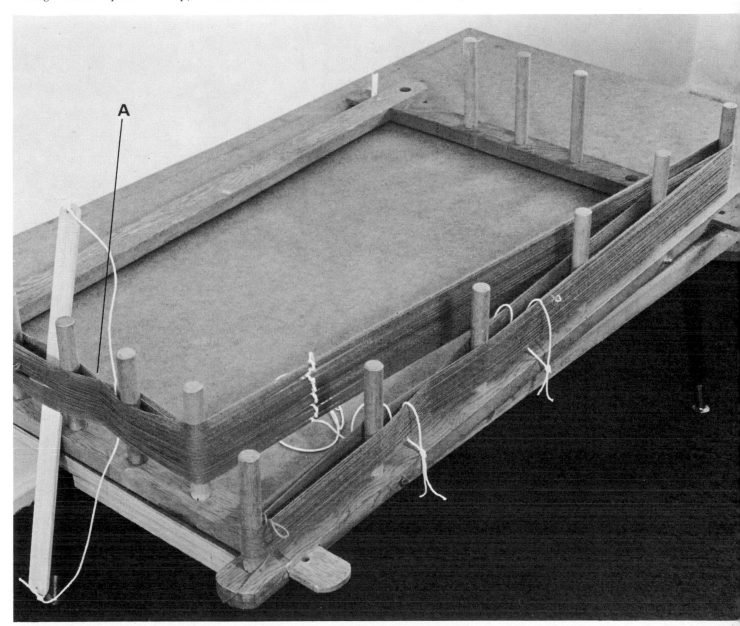

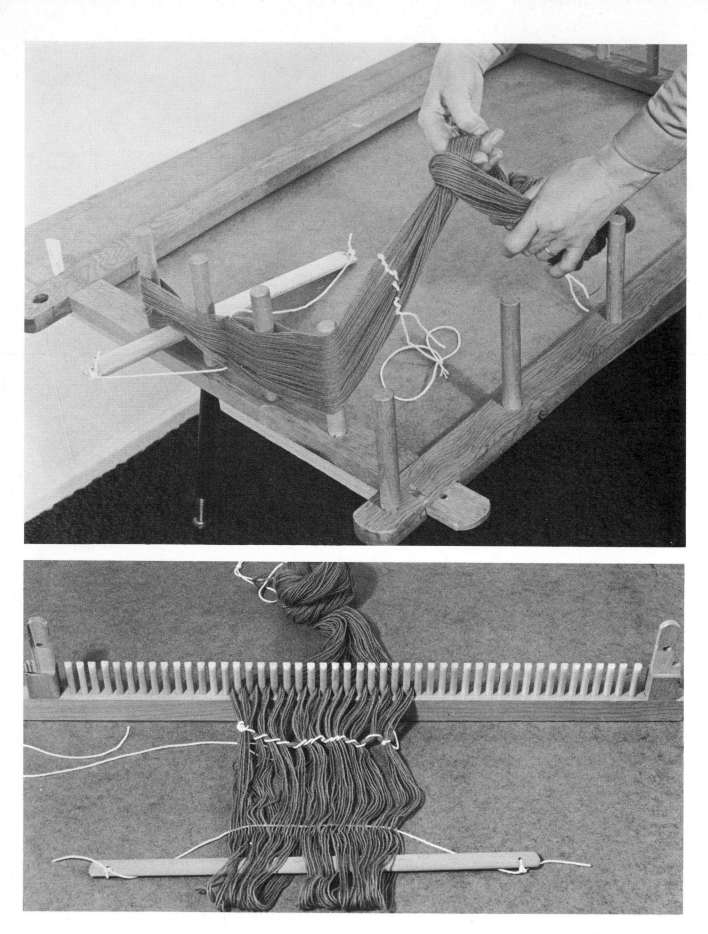

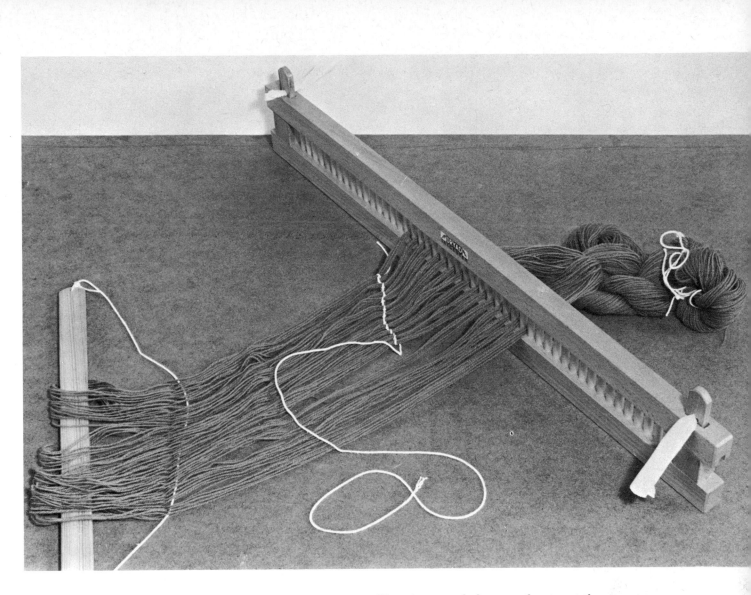

Fig. A–4. Chaining a warp with two crosses (opposite above).

Fig. A–5. The warp has been raddled 16 dent, with two groups of 8 to the inch, using the bunches of 8 threads marked during warping (opposite below).

Fig. A–6. The warp is held securely in the raddle with the top fastened. Now the marker cord is removed (above).

Finishing Woollen Fabrics (Milling). Washing woollen cloth is very important, particularly if you are using oily singles tweed yarns. When washed, the cloth loses the stiffness caused by the oil in the wool, and the yarn fibres open to fill the spaces between warp and weft.

Before washing, measure the piece of cloth. Then wash it in hand-hot water with soapflakes, *squeezing the fabric gently in the suds.* Long lengths of cloth can be finished in the bath in a minimum of water and plenty of soapflakes. Tread the cloth with your feet if it is too big to do by hand. Use a water softener if you live in a hard water area.

It is not easy for a beginner to know when the cloth is sufficiently *milled. The yarn is expanded enough when warp and weft no longer slip on each other.* To continue washing after this stage will make the cloth mat together and begin to felt.

Rinse in several changes of water at the same temperature as the washing water, making sure that no soap remains in the cloth. Don't wring, but *spin very lightly or squeeze the water out gently.* While still damp, roll the cloth on a slatted roller. This is a special roller made specifically for the purpose of drying milled cloth, but if you do not wish to buy one, use a broom handle and roll the cloth on to it with a towel between each layer. Leave it for two days, then unroll it and wind on the other way. Take care to *keep the selvedges level, and make sure the weft lies straight across the roller.* Leave until dry. Short pieces can be pinned out on a board on towels, but *be careful not to distort the edges* by pulling too much on the fabric before you pin. Don't be tempted to speed up the drying by putting the cloth in hot sunshine or over a radiator. *Let it dry naturally.*

When the cloth is dry it should not need pressing. Measure it again and note how much length and width it has lost in finishing. This will help you calculate future quantities. An average loss in woollens is 3 in. in every 36 in., both in length and width.

When planning a woollen warp always make sure you allow extra length and width to compensate for shrinkage of the cloth in finishing. At least 10 per cent should be added to warp length and width.

101

Fig. A–7. The warp tied on to the back of the loom with the stick through one loop of the second cross (below).

Fig. A–8. Beaming the warp. Covering the knots in the back tie-up with warp sticks (opposite above).

Fig. A–9. The warp has been wound on. Now the cross sticks are placed between the marked layers of warp at the cross (opposite below).

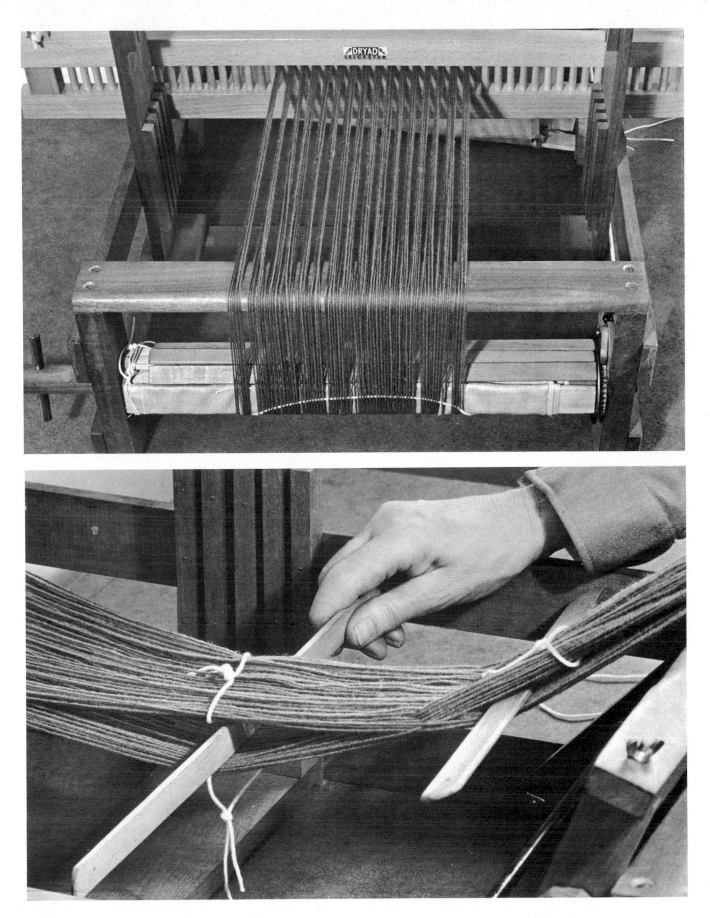

Appendix B
Weaving on Rings

(Figs. 1–1, 1–2 and 1–3.)
Tie on one side of the ring and pass the yarn round the ring before taking it across to the other side. Wrap round the opposite side and return across the ring. This wrapping between each thread across the ring spaces the warp and keeps it firm.

The wind chimes in Fig. 1–3 were woven in lime and white plastic raffia on a synthetic chenille warp. Weaving started at the small ring at the top. After an inch the warp was woven in slit technique, some warp threads being left unwoven.

Appendix C
Estimating Weight of Yarn for Warp and Weft

Multiply the warp width by ends per inch, and add any extra selvedge threads. The number arrived at, multiplied by the length of the warp in yards, divided by the count of the yarn, will give the total weight of the yarn in pounds. For small amounts multiply by 16 to convert to ounces.

$$\frac{\textit{Warp}}{\text{ends per inch} \times \text{width of warp in ins.} \times \text{length in yds.}}{\text{no. of hanks per lb. (count)} \times \text{no. of yds. in each hank}}$$

$$\textit{Weft}$$
$$\frac{\text{picks per inch} \times \text{length to be woven in ins.} \times \text{width of warp in yds.}}{\text{no. of hanks per lb. (count)} \times \text{no. of yds. in each hank}}$$

Fig. D–1. Home-made loom from scrap wood.

Appendix D
A Simple Home-Made Loom

Here is a simple 2-way loom to be used with the rigid heddle, as in Fig. 1–4. It was made from scraps of wood found in the toolshed, and the only tools used were a saw, a drill and a screwdriver. The only critical dimension is the inside width, which must be sufficient for the heddle used. This loom uses a 15 in. heddle, and is 9 in. high.

Joints can be simple halvings or just screwed together. Take care that the loom is square and rigid. The front and back rollers were made from an old broom handle. One inch holes were drilled half-way through one side of the loom and completely through the other. The roller is located by a small scrap of dowel pressed into a hole, as can be seen in Fig. D–1. Tension is obtained at each end of the loom by means of holes bored through the diameter of the protruding part of the roller through which a nail or meat skewer can be placed to lock against the screws. This is shown in detail in Figs. D–2 and D–3.

To finish, tack a piece of firm cotton or linen to each roller to make the apron. The free end of the cloth should have a hem in it big enough to take a warp stick. Punch 5 holes through the cloth close to the hem. These are for the pieces of string which will be used to make the tie-up. Cut

Fig. D–2. Detail of home-made loom, showing its locking device.

each piece 20 in. long. Fold the string in half and put the loop formed through the hole in the apron. Then pass the free ends through the loop, forming a lark's head knot.

The Dryad rigid Metlyx heddle used with this loom is available in the United States from the Craftool Co., 1421 West 240th Street, Harbor City, Calif. 90710 (see *Suppliers*).

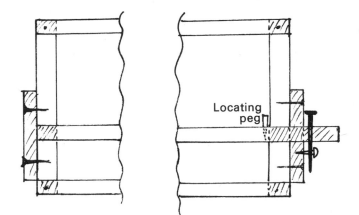

Fig. D–3. Cross-section of home-made loom, seen from the front, showing the broom handle roller and the locking device.

Appendix E
The 2-Way Loom with 2 Shafts and a Reed

Looms are available with 2 shafts and a separate reed. These looms are more versatile in use than rigid heddle looms, and more interesting work can be undertaken, since the separate reed makes a variety of denting possible. However, patterns cannot be woven.

As there are only 2 shafts, the warp strands are threaded through the heddle eye of each frame alternately. Threading the reed and the front tie-up are the same as with a 4-shaft loom. Weaving is done by raising each shaft in turn and beating with the reed.

Appendix F
The Foot Power Loom

A foot power loom is quicker to use than a table loom. A continuous rhythm in weaving soon becomes automatic, as the hands are free to throw the shuttle and swing the batten, while the feet work the pedals to move the shafts. Undoubtedly this loom is a good choice if you plan to weave longer lengths of cloth, perhaps to sell. As it is a more complicated piece of machinery than a table loom, it is more expensive, and more space is needed to house it.

The *treadles or pedals* are attached to *lams* (horizontal bars of wood under the shafts). These in turn are tied to the *harnesses,* so that when the feet operate the treadles the lams assist the direct pull on each shaft to make a clear shed. Early looms had no lams – the pedals were tied directly to the shafts. There are more treadles than shafts, making possible a variety of combinations of tie-up. In 4-harness looms there are usually 6 pedals. The 2 inside pedals are usually tied to 1 and 3 and 2 and 4, for plain weave. In twill, the outside 2 pedals at each side are tied to make the 4 picks of 2/2 twill.

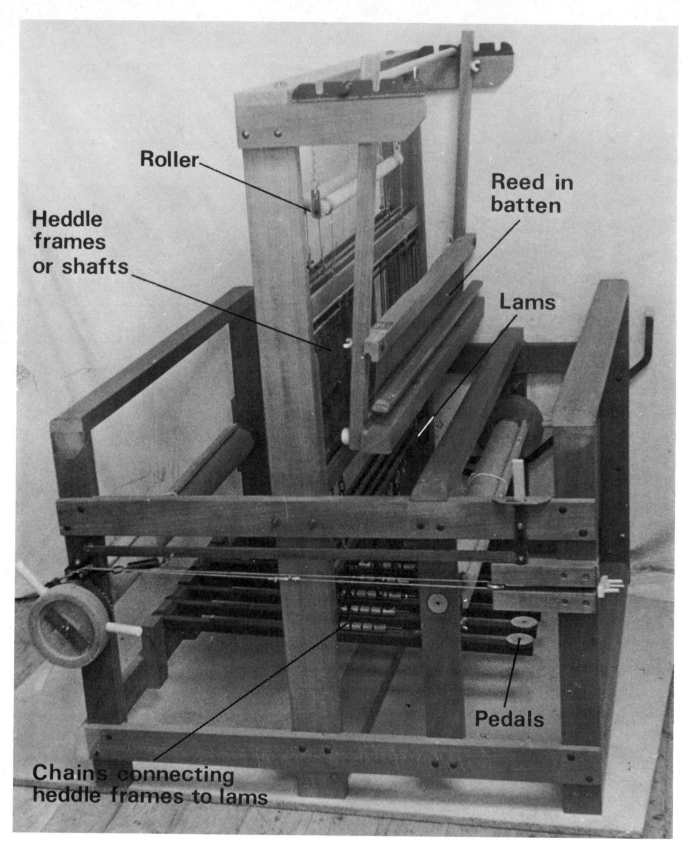

Roller

Reed in batten

Heddle frames or shafts

Lams

Chains connecting heddle frames to lams

Pedals

Fig. F–1. Harris foot power loom, de luxe model. Chains and rollers suspend the heddle shafts or frames. Chains and slipbolts are used to connect frames, lams and pedals. The shed for weaving is made by pressing the pedals with your feet.

From the right
Tie shafts 1 and 2 to pedal 1
Tie shafts 3 and 2 to pedal 2
Tie shafts 1 and 3 to pedal 3 ⎫ These are the pedals
Tie shafts 2 and 4 to pedal 4 ⎭ for plain weave
Tie shafts 4 and 3 to pedal 5
Tie shafts 1 and 4 to pedal 6

The *mounting*, i.e. the ways in which the shafts are moved, varies according to the particular loom. Some looms have a *rising shed*, while in others one set of warp threads is raised while the other set is lowered. The way in which the pedals pivot also varies. The batten holding the reed can be top slung or underslung, i.e. connected to the side of the loom.

The connections between the shafts, lams and pedals are usually made of loom cord but some makers use chains. This takes away some of the difficulties of adjustment that a beginner would find difficult.

Some makers include a built-in stool, at the correct height for comfort, with their looms. If you are considering buying a large item like this, look at as many as you can before you decide. Most loom manufacturers are enthusiasts and will offer sound advice. Buy as large a loom as you can afford (and can house!), and make sure you do not need to rise from your seat to let out more warp from the back roller and adjust the front roller.

The same instructions for making and threading a warp on table looms apply to foot looms. Adequate loom wastage for a foot loom would be an extra yard on the warp length. Clear space for beaming the warp by moving the heddles to each side on the shafts or by removing the whole mounting. The reed in its batten should be taken off the loom for threading.

The only real difference in procedure is the tie-up of pedals to lams and shafts. *The Technique of Weaving* by John Tovey (see *Recommended Books*) deals with this well.

Appendix G
The Tex System

The Tex system of classifying yarns is a new international scheme, which is intended eventually to replace all the different systems in use today. It is expected to be in operation in Great Britain soon, possibly by 1975. Tex is the weight in grammes of 1 kilometre (1000 metres) of yarn. It is a direct system starting from weighing a set unit length (1 kilometre). This means that if 1 kilometre of the yarn weighs 10 grammes the Tex count of that yarn will be 10. A higher number means a thicker yarn, and a lower number a finer one. This is the direct opposite of the traditional British system, where the indirect system for cotton is based on length per unit weight; in indirect systems the thicker the yarn, the lower the number.

Tex will be introduced gradually in three stages. To begin with, both systems will be marked on yarns, the Tex count after the old numbering system. After Tex has been used for some time, the old numbers will be put in parentheses after the Tex number. Finally only the Tex number will be shown.

Appendix H
Imperial to Metric Conversion

Measurements in this book have been given in inches only, since the metric system at present shows no signs of replacing Imperial measurements in weaving (apart from the Tex yarn numbering system described in Appendix G). Measurements and calculations in inches can, if necessary, quickly be converted to centimetres by multiplying by 2·5.

Standard reeds in Britain and the United States are in dents per inch, while metric reeds are in dents per 10 cm. It is assumed that readers will be using an Imperial reed, and the denting has therefore been worked out to fit the standard reed (i.e. in inches). To convert to metric, multiply the number of dents per inch by 4 to obtain dents per 10 cm.

Glossary of Terms Used in Weaving

Apron
A length of strong cotton or linen cloth attached to the front and back rollers of the loom, to which the warp is tied.

Balanced Weave
A weave in which there are an equal number of warp threads to the inch as there are weft rows of weaving. Also known as a 50/50 fabric.

Back Beam or Warp Beam
The roller at the back of the loom, to which the warp is tied.

Batten
A swinging wooden frame carrying the reed. It is pivoted to the top or side of the loom.

Beaming
See *Rolling On.*

Beater
Another name for the *reed.* This is a metal or wooden tool with evenly spaced openings or *dents* through which successive warp threads are threaded. It is used (a) to space the warp, and (b) to beat the picks of weft to make the cloth firm.

Binder
A weft of tabby or plain weave used to bind down between each pick of pattern weaving using long weft floats. A binder may be used between each row in a multiple pick.

Bobbin
A small wooden spool held in a shuttle, on which weft thread is wound.

Bobbin Winder
A device for winding spools.

Chaining
A method of removing the warp from a warping board or warping posts, similar to making a chain of crochet. This keeps the warp untangled.

Cheese
A round package of yarn.

Cone
A conical package of yarn.

Count
A system of numbering yarns according to the relationship between the yarn's weight and its length.

Cross
The figure-eight-shaped interlacing of threads in a warp which keeps the threads in their correct order.

Cross Sticks or Shed Sticks
Two sticks of the same length which are used to hold the cross threads in position.

Cut
A term used in numbering the thickness of tweed singles yarn.

Dent
A vertical space or slit in the reed, through which the warp threads pass, singly or in pairs or in groups. Reeds vary in the number of dents to the inch, and are classified from fine to coarse.

Draft
A diagram on squared paper showing a weaving pattern.

End
One single warp thread.

Entering
Threading the warp ends through the eyes of the heddles. Known also as threading or drawing in.

Eye or Mail
A small loop or hole in the centre of each heddle to hold the warp end.

Fell
The last pick of weaving, beaten up.

Fibre
The natural or synthetic materials from which yarns are made.

Finishing, Fulling or Milling
Washing and drying of cloth after weaving.

Fixed or Rigid Heddle
(See *Heddle.*) A device for holding warp threads at equal distances from one another in a 2-way loom. It consists of a length of metal or wood cut into a series of vertical strips with holes in the middle of them. There are spaces between these strips. When entering the warp, one end goes through the hole in the rigid strip and the next end goes in the space between the strips. When the heddle is raised, with the warp taut, those ends which are through the holes are held in the one position and must rise with the heddle. The other ends, in the spaces, will sink. Thus a space is formed through which the shuttle carrying the weft thread is passed.
   The opposite *shed* is made by pushing the rigid heddle down.

Four-Shaft Loom, 4-Way Loom or 4-Harness Loom
A loom with 4 sets of heddles mounted on frames, on which patterns can be woven.

Fulling
See *Finishing*.

Hank
An 840 yard length used in the count of cotton.

Heald
Another name for a *heddle*.

Heddle
A length of string or metal with a central loop, the eye, which holds a warp end. There are loops at each end of the heddle, and it hangs by these loops from the horizontal bars of the frame.

Heddle Clamp or Block
Two pieces of wood between which the rigid heddle is clamped by wing nuts to hold it rigid while the warp is threaded through it.

Lam or March
A bar or lever hung between pedals and shafts on a foot power loom. The pedals are tied to the shafts through the lams.

Lea
A length of 300 yards used in the count of linen.

Loom
Any device on which a warp may be stretched and weft interlaced to make cloth.

Mail
See *Eye*.

Milling
See *Finishing*.

Overshot or Float
This occurs when a weft thread passes over several warp ends. Some patterns also contain warp floats.

Pawl
A movable metal tongue which falls into the teeth on the *ratchet wheel* at the front and back of the loom to prevent the rollers moving.

Pick
One passage of the shuttle carrying a weft thread from selvedge to selvedge, i.e. one row of weaving.

Quill
Another name for a *bobbin*.

Raddle
A wooden comb-like device with a removable top and wooden pegs set at equal intervals. It is used for spread-

ing out the warp to its correct width, according to *dent*.

Ratchet
A wheel with teeth cut into it, used in conjunction with a *pawl*.

Reed
A metal comb, originally made from reeds, with vertical grooves in it. It is used for spacing the warp and beating up the picks of weaving.

Reeding or Sleying
Entering the warp in the reed.

Reed Hook
A flat metal hook for threading the reed.

Rigid Heddle
See *Fixed Heddle*.

Rolling On or Beaming
The action of rolling the warp, held to its correct width in the raddle, on the back of the loom.

Rolling On Sticks
See *Warp Sticks*.

Selvedge
The woven edge of the cloth.

Sett
The number of warp ends to the inch.

Shed
The triangular space formed when a warp is divided into 2 layers by the action of heddles. The shuttle, carrying the weft, passes through the shed.

Shed Sticks
See *Cross Sticks*.

Shot
A pick or row of weaving.

Shuttle
The tool for carrying the weft. The simplest one is a flat stick with a shaped end. A boat or roller shuttle contains a bobbin on to which the weft yarn is wound.

Shuttle Race
A narrow shelf at the front of the batten holding the reed, along which the boat or roller shuttle runs.

Singles
A single continuous yarn, unplied.

Sleying
See *Reeding*.

Take-up
The amount of length a yarn 'loses' when it is woven in and out to form cloth. There is both warp and weft take-up.

Threading Hook
Similar to a fine crochet hook, used for entering the warp on the heddles.

Tie-Up
The way the shafts are connected to the pedals through the lams on a foot power loom. Also the tie-up of warp to the front of the loom.

Twist
The way the fibres twist in a yarn, e.g. S twist or Z twist.

Two-Way Loom
A simple loom with (a) a rigid heddle for spacing and beating, or (b) 2 shafts and a reed.

Warp
The lengthwise-running threads which are stretched on a loom.

Warp Beam
See *Back Beam*.

Warp Faced Cloth
Cloth where more warp shows on the surface than weft.

Warp Sticks or Rolling On Sticks
Narrow flat sticks used between successive rounds of warp on the back roller. Used also to attach the warp to the *aprons* at the front and back of the loom.

Warping Frame
A wooden frame set with movable pegs for warping.

Warping Mill
A cylindrical frame for making longer warps.

Warping Posts
Single or double pegs set in wooden blocks. These are clamped to a table and a warp is made on them.

Weft
The threads which interlace the warp across the cloth.

Weft Faced Cloth
Cloth where more weft shows on the surface than warp.

Recommended Books

Weaving

The Technique of Weaving, John Tovey. Batsford, London, and Van Nostrand Reinhold, New York, 1965.
The Art of Weaving, Else Regensteiner. Studio Vista, London, and Van Nostrand Reinhold, New York, 1970.
The Weaver's Book, Harriet Tidball. Macmillan, New York, 1961.
The Weaver's Craft, L. E. Simpson and M. Weir. Dryad Press, Leicester, 1963.
Handloom Weaving, Plain and Ornamental, L. Hooper. Pitman, Bath, 1936.
New Key to Weaving, M. Black. Bruce, Milwaukee, 1957.
Weaving is Fun, Jean Wilson. Studio Vista, London, and Van Nostrand Reinhold, New York, 1971.
Your Hand Weaving, Elsie Davenport. Craft and Hobby Book Service, California.

Other Techniques

Macramé, the Art of Creative Knotting, Virginia Harvey. Van Nostrand Reinhold, London and New York, 1967.
Tie and Dye Made Easy, Anne Maile. Mills and Boon, London, 1971.
Creating with Batik, Ellen Bystrom. Van Nostrand Reinhold, London and New York, 1974.
The Bead Book: Sewing and Weaving with Beads, I. Erlandsen and H. Mooi. Van Nostrand Reinhold, London and New York, 1974

Suppliers

Great Britain

Looms and Equipment
Harris Looms Limited, Northgrove Road, Hawkhurst, Kent
(metric as well as Imperial reeds.)

Dryad, Northgates, Leicester.

Yarns
Dryad, Northgates, Leicester.

T. M. Hunter, Sutherland Wool Mills, Brora, Sutherland.

Yarns, 21 Portland Street, Taunton, TA1 1UY.

The Rug-Craft Centre, Dept. W, Croft Mill, Hebden Bridge, HX7 8AP.

William Hall & Co. Ltd., 177 Stanley Road, Cheadle Hulme, Cheadle, Cheshire, SK8 6RF
(Swedish linen yarns; the firm is the sole U.K. distributor of Berga handweaving wool and Ryagarn.)

All the above suppliers will send price lists and catalogues on request.

Dyes
Mayborn Products Ltd., Dylon Works, Sydenham, London S.E.26
(Procion dyes.)

M. E. McCreary & Co., 815 Lisburn Road, Belfast, Northern Ireland
(Polyprint pigment dyestuffs.)

Dylon dyes are available from ironmongers and general and department stores.

Decorative Items
Hobby Horse, 15–17 Langton Street, London S.W.10
(bead looms, beads, macramé yarn and shells for wind chimes.)

Ells & Farrier Ltd., 5 Princes Street, Hanover Square, London W.1
(bead looms, sequins and beads.)

S. E. Cuming, 64 Margaret Street, London W.1
(beads.)

United States and Canada

Looms and Equipment
The Craftool Co., 1421 West 240th Street, Harbor City, Calif. 90710
(Dryad looms and accessories.)

For names and addresses of local Harris agents, write to the British address of Harris Looms Limited.

Yarns
Fiber to Fabric, 317 4th Street, Kirkland, Washington 98033

Lily Mills, Dept. HWH, Shelby, North Carolina 28150

Magnolia Weaving, 2635 29th West Seattle, Washington 98199

Greentree Ranch Wools, 163 North Carter Lake Road, Loveland, Colorado 80537

Nilus LeClerc Inc., L'Islet, Quebec, Canada

Robin and Russ Handweavers, 533 North Adams Street, McMinneville, Oregon

The Yarn Depot Inc., 545 Sutter Street, San Francisco, Calif. 94102

Dyes
Dupont de Nemours Co. Inc., 50 Page Road, Clifton, New Jersey

ICI Organics Inc., 55 Canal Street, Providence, Rhode Island 02901

Farquahar Fabric Dyes, Box 1008, Station A, Toronto 116, Canada

Decorative Items
Robin and Russ Handweavers
(address above; macramé yarn.)

The Yarn Depot Inc.
(address above; macramé yarn.)

Sidney Coe Inc., 65 West 37th Street, New York, NY
(beads, pearls, novelties.)

Arareity, 1021 R Street, Sacramento, California
(rare and wooden beads.)

Index

Figures in *Italics* refer to illustrations